Father Jimmy

Father Jimmy

The Life and Times of Father Jimmy Tompkins

Jim Lotz and Michael R. Welton

Breton Books
Wreck Cove, Cape Breton Island
1997

Editor: Ronald Caplan
Production Assistance: Bonnie Thompson
Composition: Glenda Watt

For photographs, our thanks to St. Francis Xavier University
Archives; Tompkins Memorial Library, Reserve Mines;
Drs. Coady & Tompkins Memorial Library, Margaree Forks;
National Film Board of Canada; Beaton Institute, University
College of Cape Breton; Archives of the Sisters of Saint
Martha; and the personal collection of Sister Stella Chafe.

THE CANADA COUNCIL | LE CONSEIL DES ARTS
FOR THE ARTS | DU CANADA
SINCE 1957 | DEPUIS 1957
We acknowledge the support of
the Canada Council for the Arts for our publishing program.

We also gratefully acknowledge support from Cultural Affairs, Nova Scotia Department of Education and Culture

Canadian Cataloguing In Publication Data

Lotz, Jim, 1929-

    Father Jimmy.

    Includes bibliographical references.
    ISBN 1-895415-23-3

1. Tompkins, James J., 1870-1953. 2. Antigonish Movement — History. 3. Priests — Nova Scotia — Biography. I. Welton, Michael Robert, 1942- II. Title.

BX4705.T68L67 1997   307.1'4'092   C97-950143-1

CONTENTS

PHOTOGRAPHS between pages 42 and 43.

INTRODUCTION

"He was a wound-up alarm clock of God's love!"

George Boyle

THIS BOOK TELLS THE STORY of the life and times of Father James John Tompkins—"Father Jimmy"—the spiritual founder of the Antigonish Movement.

Born in the Margaree Valley of Cape Breton in 1870, he died in Antigonish in 1953. This small, dynamic Nova Scotian taught school to pay his way through Saint Francis Xavier University in Antigonish, and then became a priest. Ordained in 1902, Father Jimmy returned to St. F.X. as professor and administrator. He began to urge that university to help ordinary people—the "little fellows"—to understand the forces affecting them and to make better lives for themselves through adult education and local cooperation.

In 1921, Father Jimmy published his seminal document on adult education in Canada—*Knowledge for the People*. He also vigorously promoted the cause of university amalgamation in the Maritimes, and paid for that with exile from St. F.X., sent as parish priest to Canso. Here he put his ideas into action, stirring up the fishermen to protest and to make better lives for their families by cooperative effort. In 1935, he moved to Reserve

1

Mines and encouraged a group of miners to build their own houses, working together. These men named their new community "Tompkinsville."

He fought for regional libraries for all of Nova Scotia. He received an honorary Doctor of Laws from Dalhousie University (1919) and an honorary Master of Arts from Harvard (1941).

Father Jimmy's words and ideas are as vital to our time as they were to his. They point the way to community development through cooperation and adult education, and are at the root of the Antigonish Movement, which has touched and inspired the poorest of the poor, and thousands of others in Canada and throughout the world.

PROLOGUE

The Exiled Priest

"I am just a voice crying in the wilderness."

Father Jimmy Tompkins

IN LATE DECEMBER, 1922, four priests stood on the dock at Mulgrave on the Strait of Canso, the body of water separating Cape Breton Island from mainland Nova Scotia. Three of them had come to bid farewell to the fourth, Father James J. Tompkins. At the age of fifty-two, he had been ejected from his post as vice-president of Saint Francis Xavier University (St. F.X., in Antigonish, Nova Scotia) and sent into exile by his bishop for disturbing the tranquillity of life there by promoting the idea of university amalgamation in the Maritimes. He was sent to a new job, a new career for which he had no training or experience—priest in an impoverished fishing community.

The coastal steamer *S.S. Robert G. Cann* would take Father Jimmy to Canso. He had written a few days earlier:

"I have been turned out into the wilderness to a place called Canso...a terrible place I understand where among other things, the sun is not seen for nine months of the year on account of fog."

3

Father Jimmy—a name he disliked but by which he was universally known—stood only five feet four inches (162 centimetres) tall, and had always looked frail. Sharp-faced, with a nose like a knife blade, the priest had a firm jaw, wide mouth, large ears and small, light blue eyes. His voice, high-pitched and squeaky, had an almost querulous sound. He had used it, and his considerable writing skills, to attack a wide range of targets that he blamed for the depressed state of eastern Nova Scotia and its people.

Of politicians, he wrote:

"We have such a contemptible lot of penny half penny politicians around here that it is simply disgusting. They have for so long confided in their own infallibility and in their ability to fool the people and look wise for their own profit that they can't understand how anybody should arise to disturb their peaceful slumber."

Of his colleagues at St. F.X., Father Jimmy lamented:

"Most of our present professorial riffraff have not had even a decent high school education. There is no doubt about it that many poor innocent Catholics are having their legs pulled by educational bluffers...."

Nor did the members of his own faith escape censure:

"I believe the time is ripe for a campaign among Catholics to take their place as citizens in this country and to give up peeping through keyholes and around corners wondering who is trying to poison them. If Catholics could be cured on this score a great advance would be made."

The priest's comments on business and banks could have been written today:

"The partisan in industry cares only that men live and work at the lowest possible wage and for the smallest possible return for the product of their labor.... Thousands of branch banks skim the cream from our towns and hamlets, leaving the skim milk for local consumption. No profits are distributed locally.... The country is impoverished for the benefit of monopolizers in the great centers....

"Industrially and financially we are living under a despotism. Our money and our resources should not be handed over to any group or class, no matter how benevolent or however inspired by high purpose, because it is not good for the country—and it is not democratic. It is the very opposite of democracy."

Joe Laben, a Cape Breton coal miner who with Father Jimmy's guidance became a pioneer and leader in cooperative housing, said of him:

"He was such a pest up at the college [Saint Francis Xavier]. He criticized everything that was going on. He wanted to have a simple form of education.... He was after the bishop. 'Fellows down there are all going communist, they're starving— why don't we do something for them?' The bishop wouldn't move—then he *did* move. He sent Father Tompkins to Dover, a little place in Canso, the poorest parish in the diocese. He punished him."

This turbulent priest did not simply criticize the existing system. He also offered a vision of a new and better life for the poor, and had a deep faith in the ability of ordinary people to help themselves. Father Jimmy wrote:

"The old idea conceived of education as a 'ladder,' the top rung of which a scanty 5 percent might endeavour to reach but from which 95 percent of the people were barred because there was, as a matter of fact, no room on it for them. The new idea of education represents it as a broad 'highway' along which all men would be encouraged to travel abreast as far as their powers can carry them. Let us have done with 'ladders' and take our stride on the broad 'highway.'"

His own university, St. F.X., took the brightest of the local youth, educated them in traditional academic ways, and gave them credentials—then saw many of them leave the region. This outmigration increased as times became tougher in eastern Nova Scotia after the First World War. Father Jimmy believed that educated ordinary people who *stay* were the key to revitalizing the region and creating prosperity for all.

In 1920, Father Jimmy spoke about the promise of education and organization for creating the good life:

"The wage system is degenerating into industrial anarchy before our very eyes.... The worker must be made a partner so that he may get a proper share of the income earned by his work.... Conditions would be remedied only by the people rising to an appreciation of the seriousness of the situation and setting their intelligence to seek a rational solution....

"Education I should put down as the first and most necessary remedy—education in the broadest and most comprehensive sense. Effective organization can only come where there is highly trained intelligence...from among men in whom moral and intellectual virtue has been fostered."

Tompkins believed that such men—and women—could be found among the ordinary working people. Ida Delaney, who helped to put his ideas into practice, recalled his words: "Adult education must be prepared to find truth where it finds it: it must also be prepared to accept talent where it finds it."

Although Father Jimmy attracted some remarkable women to his cause, he concentrated most of his efforts on encouraging leadership in men. He sought them out, forcing them to think for themselves about their problems and how they could solve them with their own resources.

As a friend put it, "Father Jimmy wouldn't even let out the cat for you. But he'd stay up half the night nagging *you* to do it."

A journalist added, "He was a terrible nagger to try to get people to do things, insisting that you read things. If you didn't get the book, he would get it and would almost sit there until you read it."

ONE OF THE OTHER FOUR PRIESTS on the Mulgrave dock was Moses Michael Coady, Father Jimmy's cousin. Physically, the two men could not have been more different. Coady was large, craggy-featured, and impressive; he had a commanding Irish voice, nothing like his cousin's. Coady had seen no choice for Tompkins but to accept the bishop's decision, to go. Years later, in an appreciation of Tompkins, he wrote:

"Dr. Tompkins' greatness is of the kind that defies classification by all ordinary rules.... He was a personality of many facets. His dynamism, his overpowering mental activity, his tenacity overcompensated for his frail physique.... He was a persistent purveyor of ideas and an inspirer of others. He achieved this by continuous self-education, by prodding, personal contact and innumerable letters to those whom he felt would best promote those ideas.

"Paradoxically, although he was a widely educated man and a citizen of the world...when he became possessed of an idea...he pursued it with a singleness of purpose that would not be deflected. This characteristic was both a strength and a weakness. He could be illogical when an idea dominated him; but in general, he had a genius for knowing the proper thing to do and doing it at the right time."

Coady and Tompkins were destined to be the leaders of the Antigonish Movement, a worldwide cooperative movement neither of them could have envisioned on that dark, defeated December day.

The Antigonish Movement is a world-famous social action venture, too often forgotten or mythologized in Canada today. Using adult education methods, it encouraged fishermen, farmers, miners and others to establish study clubs. From these sprang credit unions and cooperatives that gave working class people more control over their social and economic destinies.

CHAPTER ONE

The Passionate Educator

"Ideas have hands and feet. They'll do work for you. You have to give the people ideas. Then they'll blow the roof off!"

Father Jimmy Tompkins

THE HOUSE IN WHICH James John Tompkins grew up still stands in Cape Breton Island, Nova Scotia—a plain wooden farmhouse about four kilometres from Margaree Forks, overlooking the Margaree River in Inverness County.

The Tompkins family arrived from Wexford, Ireland, in 1829. Four brothers and a sister carved a small farm from the forest in North East Margaree. The Coadys, another Irish family, settled nearby at Margaree Forks. The land was fertile and salmon ran in the river, but self-sufficient farm life proved to be hard, year-round work.

The Tompkins and the Coadys intermarried. Two of the children would reshape life in Nova Scotia, launching a social movement that touched and inspired thousands of people worldwide.

In 1870, when James was seven months old, his mother, Judith Coady, became ill, was never well afterward. The child was taken by his grandmother to live with the Coadys. Judith had three more sons and then died. James' father, John, remarried, but the boy did not return to live with his family. The small, frail James grew to manhood among the twelve tall and robust Coady children.

The self-sufficient life had begun to fade in rural Nova Scotia. Life on the land could not sustain the settlers' descendants, and many farms were simply abandoned. Sons and daughters left to work in the "Boston States" or sought their fortune out west. Others were tempted to Sydney and other towns that had grown up around coal mines and steel mills, demanding labour at the end of the nineteenth century.

For an ambitious youth who did not want to follow these paths, education offered a few more opportunities. Young Tompkins walked daily to Joe Boyle's school at Margaree Forks. He showed no interest in sports but learned to use his fists to defend himself. In 1886, he travelled to Chéticamp, an Acadian community on the west coast of Cape Breton, to help his uncle Pat Coady, a teacher.

Chéticamp was dominated by Father Pierre Fiset, the dynamic parish priest who came there in 1875. The stamp of his powerful presence was everywhere. One of several activist priests in the Maritimes—such as Abbé Belcourt of Rustico, PEI, who organized the first "people's bank" in North America in 1862—Fiset *might* have served as Tompkins' first example of how one priest could make a real difference in people's lives. Born to wealth in Québec, Father Fiset served—and ruled—in Chéticamp for thirty-four years. A simple man who welcomed the poor as well as the prominent to his table, this remarkable priest had strong entrepreneurial instincts.

When Acadians first settled in Cape Breton, merchants from the English Channel island of Jersey took control of the fishing industry. The fishermen of Chéticamp bought what they needed and sold what they caught to *les Jersiais*. Their situation was similar to that of many other people who worked the land and the sea in eastern Nova Scotia. Having never developed their own merchant class, they were prey to exploitation by outsiders who reaped most of the benefits of their hard work.

Father Fiset was determined to break the grip of these middlemen who controlled the lives of his people. The fact that *les Jersiais* were Protestant added spice to his efforts in local economic development. Fiset bought a store and a lobster factory, built a wharf, started a gypsum mine, and raised funds to erect the huge church whose spire still dominates the community and the coast. While he did nothing to encourage his flock to think and act for themselves, this strong-willed, able manager used his office and his own money to generate employment in Chéticamp. Fiset upset the local hierarchy, and the Jersey merchants sought, without success, to have him removed.

The conditions under which the French Acadians of Chéticamp lived could not have been lost on a young, searching Tompkins. Fiset would have been his priest while in Chéticamp, and he'd have in him an early example of the difference even one vigorous priest can make in a community. But Tompkins left no definitive record about this.

IN 1888, TOMPKINS LEFT Cape Breton to register at Saint Francis Xavier College, where room, board and tuition cost $2.75 a week. Founded in Arichat in 1853, the college moved to Antigonish two years later. While it now had about one hundred students, the small, poverty-stricken Catholic institution had barely survived. It lacked space to board all those who applied for entry and had no offices for professors. The rector, Rev. Dr. Neil McNeil, son of an Inverness County blacksmith, began an ambitious building program in 1887-88. With Bishop Cameron, head of the diocese, he secured funds for buildings, set up an endowment fund, incorporated a Board of Directors, and strengthened the faculty by hiring science teachers. By 1888, Cameron boasted that St. F.X. had been "largely instrumental in giving a bishop and sixty-four priests to the church and preparing a still larger number of edifying and intelligent laymen for the learned professions."

In its early years, the college taught the children of Scottish-Catholic fishing and farming families. By 1890, the student body began to change. Increasingly, its members came from the families of miners, merchants and professionals as the economy of Nova Scotia diversified.

For seven years, James Tompkins alternated between being a student on the campus and teaching in the small communities to pay for his education. He studied hard, showing a gift for mathematics, teaching that subject and Greek at St. F.X. after graduation.

In 1896, Tompkins decided to become a priest. Despite an archive of hundreds of letters, he left nothing that tells us why. Nearly every Catholic family sought to offer a son to the church, usually the most gifted. And often the most ambitious. But Moses Coady wrote that Tompkins "was not a climber...he had no ambition to achieve place and power among men for himself...."

At first, it looked as if poverty and poor health would keep Tompkins from becoming a priest. One account claims that an uncle, "Jim the Tanner," paid for his education, another that Bishop Cameron found the money. A sympathetic doctor gave the never-hearty Tompkins a clean bill of health, and the twenty-seven-year-old Cape Bretoner arrived in Rome to study at the Urban College of Propaganda in the first week of November, 1897.

Seminarians in Rome felt a strong, new wind blowing through the Catholic Church in the 1890s. On May 15, 1891, Pope Leo XIII issued his encyclical *Rerum Novarum—New Things*. Nineteenth- and early twentieth-century Catholicism in Europe, the United States and Canada could be described as a fortress Catholicism wherein Catholics were ghettoized, dissent was controlled and hostility to the "Protestant" and the "secular" was encouraged. Behind the fortress walls Catholic leaders hoped to ride out storms of secularism and socialism.

This document, *Rerum Novarum*, lowered the drawbridge of fortress Catholicism to the plight of suffering workers and recognized the new forces sweeping industrialized nations in the face of poverty, injustice and exploitation. The *Communist Manifesto*, first printed in German in 1848, had been translated and widely distributed among workers. Claiming that "the history of all hitherto existing society is the history of class struggles," it ended with the clarion call: "Working men of all countries, unite!"

Marx died in 1883, Engels in 1895. Their ghosts and ideas hovered over Europe as the international socialist movement, promising heaven on earth, not in the afterlife, and attracting more and more followers. New "theologies," rooted in Darwinism's survival of the fittest, rationalized ruthless, laissez-faire capitalism. In light of this, European liberalism searched for a secular, middle way to personal salvation and prosperity.

Rerum Novarum opened doors for reform-minded Catholics, calling them to action, signalling the decline of laissez-faire in their church. Catholics were encouraged to understand the forces shaping the world and to bring their faith to bear on social problems.

Pope Leo XIII asserted the rights of the family and private property against the encroachments of the state. Labour was not simply another commodity to be bought and sold; men and women had the right to just rewards for their work. The state had a duty to prevent the exploitation of workers, who had the right to form trade unions and cooperatives. In later years, Father Tompkins quoted a speaker at a meeting of Catholic bishops and priests:

"By degrees workingmen had been delivered helpless and isolated to the hard-heartedness of employers and the greed of unchecked competition;...the mischief had been increased by the rapacious usury of financiers;...to these evils was added the custom of doing work by large contracts which concentrated many branches of business in the hands of a few individuals...a small number of very rich men had been able to lay upon the teeming masses of the laboring poor a yoke little better than slavery.... The wage system is degenerating into industrial anarchy before our very eyes.... The worker must be made a partner so that he may get a proper share of the income earned by his work."

HIS DELICATE HEALTH prevented Tompkins from completing the usual doctoral degrees at the Urban College. He was not a good student; he suffered when faced with abstract philosophy. But he had found his vocation. He was ordained at the Basilica of St. John Lateran.

In turn, he influenced his cousin. He sent Moses Coady a rosary blessed by the Pope, John Henry Newman's *The Second Spring*, and a cheap edition of St. Luke's gospel. As George Boyle wrote the story, the big bell of St. Joseph's Church in Cape Breton was calling the people to Mass, while Coady was reading the "penny edition" of St. Luke. Struck with "the continuity of the same message across the centuries from the distant days of Luke,...in later life M. M. Coady looked back upon that hour (as)...the one in which he had decided to become a priest."

Father Jimmy returned to his beloved Margaree in 1902 to say his first Mass for family and friends. Then he moved to St. F.X. as professor of Greek and higher algebra, and college librarian. The university taught students in traditional academic ways, and the new professor soon became known for being self-effacing and kind, willing to tutor students needing help. His room became the centre for all the lively and radical spirits on campus. As Tompkins put it:

"Man needs two things: inspiration and courage; ideas and the putting of them into execution; ability to conceive and strength to dare. It is imperative if we are ever to get anywhere...that our whole life even from our earliest days, and particularly during our formative period, be given to noble thoughts and lofty aspirations, to reverence, purity, unselfish sacrifice for others, candor, accuracy, punctuality, and a host of other virtues that make up the ideal man.... Every young man needs to cultivate a passion, permanent and intense."

As a professor, Father Jimmy found very few ideal men at St. F.X. His university colleagues wore coats with long tails that greened with age, which he read as symbolizing their dedication to antiquated education. Tompkins said of one, "You could grow potatoes in his coat tail." He began to doubt whether such teachers would ever inspire students to become the kind of leaders needed to rescue eastern Nova Scotia from poverty.

While St. F.X. was no powerhouse of higher learning, it had shown some interesting initiatives. In 1897, it was the first Catholic institution in North America to grant degrees to women. Two years later St. F. X. established the first engineering school in Nova Scotia.

Tompkins and the reform cadre at Antigonish read *Rerum Novarum* as a text that demanded radical engagement with the pressing issues of their suffering region. *Rerum Novarum, Quadragesimo Anno* and other encyclicals were studied and debated—the minutes of their formal meetings exist— and the new spirit can be seen emerging even in *The Casket,* the conservative local newspaper. In July, 1913, *The Casket* depicted suffragettes as "wild creatures," who if given the vote "would raise problems not yet thought of...," but by October *The Casket* carried Rev. Andrew Egan's "The Catholic Church the Friend of the Working Man," calling upon Catholics to stand for the "right of the employed against injustice from all sides, and for any movement that makes for social betterment...." Father Egan's words are inexplicable outside Pope Leo XIII's epochal encyclical.

Tompkins gained a reputation as a convincing talker. The rector of St. F.X., always short of cash, used this gift to raise money. In 1905, Tompkins went to Boston to meet Neil McNeil and Dr. John Somers. The former, a fellow Cape Bretoner with little formal schooling, had moved to Massachusetts and made a fortune as a building contractor. Tompkins had to convince him that the college could help pull Nova Scotia out of the dreary dullness that Neil McNeil remembered fleeing.

Dr. Somers, born in Antigonish, had graduated from St. F.X. and felt indebted to its broad, Catholic approach to education. He had become wealthy from his practice in Boston. But he was "hardboiled," Tompkins told his friend and biographer, George Boyle. "Dr. Somers was very angry that first night. He gave me an awful drubbing.... I cultivated them [Somers and McNeil] for a long time."

Tompkins persuaded McNeil and Somers to donate money for five new buildings on the campus. He managed to set up a little sense of competition between them. He once explained that he dug ditches and waited for someone with means to fall into them! At St. F.X. he became known as a passionate educator, a persuader and a motivator.

But education was very far from the minds of most people in rural Nova Scotia and in the dirty, depressing coal and steel towns. Life here was hard for ordinary people. Every cemetery in Cape Breton contains rows of small tombstones, mute testimony to high infant mortality. Ten hours of work in a lobster factory earned young women a dollar. Families lived mainly on bread, potatoes, cabbages, salt pork, pickled mackerel and herring.

Industrial Cape Breton became the fiefdom of the Dominion Coal Company and the owners of the steel mills. Miners worked eleven- and thirteen-hour shifts, with no sickness, accident or death benefits, and could be fired without cause at any time. Before they saw their pay, the company "checked off" the men's wages: deducted payments for rent, school tax, poll tax, the church, and lamp and powder bought at the company store. After mining sixty-six tons of coal, one man took home seventy cents at the end of the month, all that remained of his total pay of $34.43.

Another miner found a single penny in the pay packet, held it up and said: "Big Pay!" After that, all his family became known as the "Big Pay Mac-Donalds," keeping alive the memory of that meagre return for a man's hard work.

The company stores provided a continual irritant, but they had some benefits, as Danny "The Dancer" MacDonald, a coal miner, recalled:

"What you got at the company store was quality and quantity. A private merchant might cut off a few ounces, but working there in the company stores was our own flesh and blood—daughters and sons of miners. If there were any breaks we got it.... But it created a way of life that wasn't good...and [during the 1925 Strike] we burned them all."

A bad system was at the root of many of the discontents of the people of eastern Nova Scotia. How could education change that? Few of the miners, fishers, or farmers had much schooling, although they knew it would benefit their children if it helped them acquire the right credentials to secure good, steady jobs. As Coady wrote:

"The bright child who gives signs of intelligence in school is immediately picked for a different career from that in which he was born. Rural people will mortgage their farms, and workers will contribute their savings to the last cent, to see that a favoured boy or girl gets a so-called chance in life....

"In our present educational procedure—which is essentially a skimming process—we are robbing our rural and industrial population of the natural leaders."

In his early, idealistic years at St. F.X., Tompkins believed that he could inspire students to remain in the region and work for its development. He hoped that the university would attract more modern teachers who shared his enthusiasm for education and learning, teachers who would help students tackle the problems besetting eastern Nova Scotia. As he wrote, "Adult education that does not issue in something practical, especially in these days of poverty and depression, has little attraction for the sons of men."

As college librarian, Tompkins had access to books and periodicals from all over the world. An avid reader, he began his lifetime practice of picking relevant passages from books, pamphlets and all kinds of publications and thrusting them at people, urging them to read *that*.

Roderick J. MacSween told the story of a group of men sitting in a store in Boisdale when "a small man came in—coat collar turned up and a scroll under his arm.... Father Tompkins asked us what we did around here. He said: 'I'm going to show you something.' He showed us the scroll that he had under his arm. It was a chart of the economic value of education, based on a report made by the Bureau of Labor Statistics, U. S. Department of Labor."

Tompkins then gave the group seated on nail kegs an informal lecture. "'I have a nice little book I would like you fellows to study.... It is by Dr. Warbasse and is called *Cooperative Development*.'" Inspired by this visit, MacSween and another fellow made plans to organize a study group in the community.

Father Tompkins had a democratic view of education:

"For us, what the people most need to learn must be what they most want to learn. Let there be the least trace of superiority or propagandism in our attitude, let the people once think of us as academic persons come to force our preconceptions upon them, and the undertaking is dead."

The priest-professor hammered away again and again at one theme:

"Ideas have hands and feet." With the right kind of education, ideas could work for people, help them to understand their problems, find solutions and "blow the roof off!"

He saw learning rooted in moral concerns:

"We shall all likely agree that there is no Catholic or Protestant Algebra. Neither is there any Catholic or Protestant way of catching and selling fish. Yet in laying the educational foundations for our movement, we insisted that to the multiplication table and its developments ought to be added the Ten Commandments and their implications."

Tompkins found allies in his passion for education. Father Michael Gillis had served as a padre with Nova Scotia's soldiers during the First World War. He had seen the comradeship, courage and self-sacrifice of men in battle and recognized the need for a moral equivalent of war that would tap the same qualities in peace. The Rev. Dr. Hugh MacPherson—"Little Doc Hugh," another ally of Tompkins in his quest to make university education practical and accessible to all—had joined the faculty of St. F.X. as professor of engineering and geology. He studied in Rome at the same time as Tompkins, describing him as "my first convert." Little Doc Hugh also did postgraduate work in science at the University of Lille. Among other things, he coached hockey and football, and one of his teams beat Harvard on its home ground. "My," he would say, "if our farmers could only have in their marketing, producing and processing, the organization we had on one of our teams! What a fine thing the rural community would become."

Little Doc Hugh went into the countryside to talk with farmers, working alongside them, impressing these men with his willingness to dirty his hands. In 1914, the provincial Department of Agriculture hired Little Doc Hugh as the first agricultural extension worker in Nova Scotia.

TOMPKINS WORKED HARD to inspire university students to stay in the region and work for the betterment of their people. In 1912 he attended a meeting in London of British universities involved in adult education, returning to Canada ablaze with a new vision: that by teaching adults the university would spark economic development and improve the lives of the people and communities of eastern Nova Scotia. Between 1913 and 1915, Tompkins spearheaded the Antigonish Forward Movement to promote this idea.

The local newspaper, *The Casket*—its name came from its self-image as a "casket of jewels"— seemed to be "anti" everything: science, communism, women's suffrage. As Father Jimmy put it in a letter in 1914: "*The Casket's* 'History of Hatred' and other things of late, have not tended to do a great deal of good either to us or to those who differ from it."

But Father Jimmy had a great capacity for seizing opportunities wherever he found them, and making good use of them. He began to write articles for *The Casket*, opening up discussions on social and economic issues, encouraging other reform-minded Catholics to contribute to the debate. They hammered away at the need to bring about change, to start dialogues with Protestants around shared concerns, to reject sectarian differences. In a letter written in 1914, Father Jimmy stated: "Our Forward Movement is decidedly a movement of the whole community, Protestant and Catholic—irrespective of politics or religion."

He had a clear idea about what the movement was all about:

"When I opened the 'Forward Movement' in *The Casket*, I made the boast that it was going to stay true if it took ten years to shake the sleep out of their bones."

And again:

"There were some people here [in Antigonish] who acted as if they thought it must have been a sin against the Holy Ghost for the people down here to wake up, have a thought of their own, or any initiative."

The priest's contempt for the politicians of his day also emerges clearly in his correspondence. Here, and in *The Casket*, his tight, taut language homed in on the region's problems.

"We have the most hopeless type of politician in Antigonish, on both sides.... It is self-interest first, votes second, the county comes in towards the foot of the list."

"Some of the bosses have been running this county to perdition—taking care of their own pockets and letting the devil look after the rest of us."

Father Jimmy did not simply puncture local pretensions, criticize the power structure, and attack attitudes inhibiting change. He saw education as the way to empower people—and kept hope alive that new ideas would permeate people's minds and energize them. He wrote in *The Casket* in 1918:

"It is high time that we make a concerted effort to put our intellectually starved workmen on the road to getting a few ideas on social questions."

And:

"A realization that institutions are changing will make people more open-minded, will make them more critical about present conditions, and will make them more susceptible to the influence of new ideas."

Between 1912 and 1922, Tompkins' espousal of adult education attracted a number of priests and lay people to what he called "Bolshevism of a Better Sort." Father Miles Tompkins, another padre, joined the reform cadre, a sort of conspiratorial elite, as mild prosperity spread in the post-war years. Father Jimmy wrote to Coady, who was studying educational theory at the Catholic University in Washington, D.C., in 1915:

"The young priests are getting welded together as never before in the history of the diocese. They are aggressive and their faces are turned toward the light. All we want now are the leaders and the enthusiasts who have got the goods to place before us. The trench digging and the spade work are practically completed."

Five years later, his enthusiasm undiminished, Father Jimmy wrote to a friend: "You can hardly imagine what a change has come over the outlook of the people through this county within the last few years. The air is recently charged with Education unrest...."

THE UNIVERSITY AND DIOCESAN hierarchy, however, showed little interest in the ideas and agitation of Tompkins. Bishop Morrison and the rector of St. F.X.—another Hugh MacPherson—wanted only peace and quiet and a steady routine in academic and clerical matters. The young continued to leave the family farms. Rural decline accelerated. Emigrants wrote home or returned on visits, telling of their new lives and new possibilities. Small country stores closed. Doctors, lawyers and other professionals moved to larger centres, as the old self-reliant way of life decayed. Tompkins pestered the university to do something about these problems, but to no avail.

Tompkins wanted the people of eastern Nova Scotia to awaken from their slumber and move into the modern world. Others sought a return to an idyllic, pastoral age. Under the leadership of the Very Rev. Donald MacAdam, the Scottish Catholic Society came into being at Iona on Cape Breton Island, July 1, 1919. MacAdam and his followers wanted to repopulate the land, inculcate in the minds of the young a regard and respect for "the dignity and independence of the farmer's life," improve rural schools and brighten the lives of young and old "by supplying the means for harmless amusement and for greater social intercourse." Society members pressured St. F.X. to provide leadership. When the university failed to take up their cause, the society began to teach Gaelic, produce plays in that language, and organize talks on church and Scottish history. Bishop Morrison viewed agrarian renewal as essential to the survival of the people of his diocese.

The basic conflict between an urge to return to the past and Father Jimmy's efforts to encourage people to take their place in the modern world became part of the background to the conflicts between Father Jimmy and his superiors that led to Tompkins' exile.

A man with an expansive, open mind and an eclectic outlook, Tompkins picked up ideas from everywhere and anywhere on how to change society. He had a magpie mind. He synthesized the bits and pieces of knowledge, and tried to determine their relevance to the local scene. Between 1912 and 1922, based at St. F.X., he developed and crystallized his philosophy of adult education.

"I am free to confess that the time has arrived when men of my class (College Professors and Clergymen)...are ready to take a more serious and enlightened interest in the problems and perplexities, the hopes and aspirations of the laboring man than they have hitherto done, not only for the good of the community but also in the interest of religion and the colleges themselves."

Tompkins and his followers had a genuine respect for the intelligence of working men and women. The British experience in adult education had shown that the traditional ways through which universities tried to meet the needs of mature people were not working. J.M. Mactavish, a wheelwright, articulated the sentiments of many intelligent and concerned members of a new class—ordinary men and women who wanted to participate in their education, not simply receive the wisdom of people who knew little of their lives and hopes—when he spoke at a meeting of academics and workers in Oxford in 1907:

"I am not here as a supplicant of my class. I decline to sit at the rich man's gate praying for crumbs. I claim for my class all the best that Oxford [University] has to give. What is the true function of a University? Is it to train the nation's best men, or to sell its gifts to the rich?"

This was the fundamental question that Tompkins and his band of "Bolsheviks of a Better Sort" kept bringing up, on and off the campus of St. F.X. Tompkins insisted that universities had to go to the people, rather than expecting them to come to it.

MEANWHILE, TOMPKINS ALSO spearheaded the enormously controversial idea of university amalgamation, the effort to create one large University of the Maritimes and Newfoundland, believing that such an arrangement would blend the religious foundations of the churchly colleges with the most modern kinds of scientific learning. He lambasted Catholic education:

"Catholics do not figure in the public life of the country because there is practically no such thing as Catholic Higher Education among us.... The people shaping the destinies of our colleges know nothing about it. They do not know what it looks like, they do not know what it is good for.... Our leaders give our people a little Latin, a little Philosophy and some Geometry, and then wonder why Catholics are not Finance Ministers and presidents of steel corporations. The world is moving forward, science is making marvellous progress, but Catholic colleges remain in the same old rut."

Expecting Catholic graduates to compete with those trained in modern institutions "is like sending an Indian to the fields of Flanders with a bow and arrow." And, he noted:

"Catholics have little to say in solving social problems, in deciding policies, in moulding the destinies of our country, because they have no centers of higher education where they can get the results of the best and latest research. This will be admitted by few 'tis true, and pity 'tis true.... As for research work, for real scholarship, there are not a dozen Catholics in Canada who could distinguish it from a gyroscope."

The answer to the problem of Catholic education lay in pooling the resources of all the universities in the Maritimes "in one or two real centers of higher education."

Tompkins wrote:

"It seems to me that what is needed in certain quarters is a little more unity, a little more Catholicism, a little less parochialism. No one section of the country can support a real university; the leaders of several sections must get together, eliminate their selfishness and jaunty self-sufficiency, and pool their resources.... If every diocese in the country were split in two...the first thing to happen would be doubling of our so-called universities. It is sad to contemplate the superfluous ease with which colleges and universities have been sprinkled over the land and the misguided zeal of local ambition to the neglect of the criterion of quality."

STORIES ABOUT FATHER JIMMY tend to paint him as a firebrand, an agitator, a disturber of peaceful and complacent ways. But he was also an excellent teacher, academic administrator and fundraiser—an able negotiator with powerful people. He became vice-president of the university in 1906, shortly after the arrival of the new rector, Rev. Dr. Hugh P. MacPherson, and he taught courses in ancient and modern languages. He constantly looked for ways to encourage a broader range of student to come to St. F.X.

Having taught in Chéticamp, he believed that

the university should do more for the Acadians in the diocese. They made up a quarter of its population, but few of them came to study at St. F.X. In October, 1919, he wrote to J.B. Bertram, secretary of the Carnegie Corporation, seeking funds to attract more Acadians by offering bursaries and superior instruction in French. He wanted the college to say to young Acadians:

"Come here and learn the best English and Science we can give you. That you may feel we are not trying to rob you of your language or traditions, we shall provide suitable and satisfactory instruction in French language and literature."

In November, 1919, the Carnegie Corporation of New York offered St. F.X. $50,000 to endow a chair in French and four bursaries. In 1920 the university succeeded in raising an equal sum for scholarships and a lectureship in education.

The connection that Father Jimmy established with the Carnegie Corporation—and the impression he made on its officials—would be lasting, supportive relationships over the years.

But when it came to university amalgamation—as with so many other ideas he wanted taken up—Tompkins did not temper his criticism with any obvious balance, such as in this case recognizing the pride Catholics felt in actually having achieved a Catholic university. In his push for amalgamation he had shown little sympathy for the impoverished university's struggle to survive on student fees and gifts—and that this was a badge of honour. Years later, his friend Sister Francis Dolores would say of him, "When he was pushing at things, he pushed too hard, he always pushed too hard"—and in the case of amalgamation he had not taken careful account of whether enough peers agreed with him.

And ironically, it was the struggle for funding to keep many independent universities and colleges alive that created the crisis.

American foundations were besieged with requests for grants from Maritime colleges. The idea of university amalgamation, centred in Halifax, emerged out of an innocent enough study by the Carnegie Corporation—trying to decide how best to place its funds. It brought to the surface suspicions and intrigue that eventually involved the Pope in Rome and, in 1922, led to Father Jimmy's exit from the university he had served so well and faithfully.

But in 1920, everything seemed to be going well for the radical professor. *Rerum Novarum* awoke some Catholic leaders from their comfortable slumber. Most slipped back into it, but not Father Tompkins! He wanted to see the word made flesh, the ideas in the encyclical put into practice. In the early '20s, Father Jimmy began to take personal initiatives to do this, not waiting for the hierarchy to act. He published a short pamphlet, *Knowledge for the People*, one of the defining documents in Canadian adult education. And he brought ordinary people onto the campus of St. F.X. to learn from the best minds he could find.

CHAPTER TWO

Knowledge for the People

"As a consequence of the war momentous changes have taken place in national life and thought. Old ways of thinking and acting have been broken up and a new spirit has gone abroad.... Nowhere is this new spirit more in evidence than in the field of education."

Father Jimmy Tompkins

THE ACHIEVEMENTS of Canada's soldiers in the First World War created a sense of national pride and unity. But the hope of a better life for all began to fade in the postwar years. In the spring of 1920 Nova Scotia began to slide into depression, with increasing unemployment, more outmigration, and even lower standards of living. On and off the campus of St. F.X., reform-minded individuals recognized that the old ways of working and living no longer worked. But how could society be changed?

Father Jimmy had an answer—adult education, and universities able to prepare the young for the changing world opportunities:

"We should be up and doing and not fritter our time away on trifles."

Tompkins criticized St. F.X. fiercely for failing to train the young to meet the demands of the modern world and to work towards creating what he called "educative democracy."

The world belonged to the specialists, technicians, experts, and professionals, and his university was not graduating such people. Tompkins' vision of "educative democracy" would give ordinary people scientific training—and strengthen their commitment to the betterment of their fellow men and women and of their communities, rather than encouraging individual paths to power and wealth.

He wrote in *The Casket*, October 30, 1919:

"By education is meant an enlightenment or intelligence effort which will show to all our adult population the possibilities which the country offers for success.... We must strike the adult population, because it is only through enlightenment that we can hope to hold what we've got, and for that matter it rests with them what type of education and how much will be given the rising generation."

Tompkins wanted to reform society. His missionary zeal came into conflict with the routines of campus life and with the diocese in this rustic setting, distant from the centres of power. Revolution, he claimed, "is only another name for reform unduly delayed." Conditions would only become better "by the people rising to an appreciation of the seriousness of the situation and by setting their intelligence to seek a rational solution."

Although an impatient man, and growing more impatient in the early 1920s, Tompkins remained a faithful Catholic. His frustration arose from what he saw as the lost promise of Catholic education.

"If we paid less attention to the imaginary 'existentia' of our philosophical text-books and more to the real 'existentia' that confronts our people in actual life we might be benefiting mankind more than we are."

And he was not kind to the clergy:

"Many of our young clergymen, as an observant layman remarked, cannot even read without exciting the laughter and pity of the average listener."

If St. F.X. did not move away from scholastic learning, the "materialists" would mold the minds of leaders. So higher education, of the right sort, "is absolutely imperative, not only to get efficiency in secular affairs, but in the long run to promote the kingdom of God."

And what kind of education did the group around Tompkins promote? At the start, their ideas were vague and idealistic. Father Jimmy:

"We select a number of dynamic ideas that are calculated to appeal to the ordinary people. I say advisedly ordinary. We have never wasted much time on the bourgeoisie. We have found that the ordinary common man is usually free from prejudices. He rarely has axes to grind, frequently has lots of ability, and is a good judge of sincerity, and gives a ready response if you have a real message."

Promoting democracy and education for solving economic problems in an academic backwater and a hierarchical setting was no easy task. And Tompkins' abrasive style and constant haranguing made his superiors and many of his fellow priests and professors uneasy. He began to sound increasingly like an Old Testament prophet and to see himself cast in this role. Scanning books, journals, pamphlets, speeches by bishops, newspapers, anything that offered ideas, examples and insights on how others were tackling a world moving towards depression, Tompkins' impatience grew. One friend described him as "volatile and eager...with a profound belief in the power of simple education." Another commented:

"He was forever urging people—everyone with whom he came into contact—to read and study and activate their minds.... He believed implicitly in the power of the people to accomplish anything if they would but awaken to the opportunities of the moment and use their collective energies in a determined effort to improve their status."

TOMPKINS STRUGGLED, in print and in person, to close the gap between activism and intellectualism. In eastern Nova Scotia, the pennies, nickels and dimes of ordinary men and women sustained

the diocese and the university. Did not these powerful institutions have a responsibility to serve those
people? Tompkins drew inspiration from the words
of Charles van Hise, president of the University of
Wisconsin, which had over forty-three thousand
learners in its adult education programs in 1919:

"The broadest ideal of service demands that
the university, as the best-fitted instrument, shall
take up the problems of carrying knowledge to the
people.... It is our aim to take out the knowledge,
whether the people ask for it or not.... We are not
going to wait for the people to come to us, we are
going to take our goods to them. We are going out to
the people."

Tompkins also found confirmation in the
words of Bishop Edward O'Dwyer of Limerick,
who deeply influenced his thinking. The Irishman
ascribed the poverty in Ireland to the lack of access
to higher education suited to the needs of the people. In a pamphlet published by the Catholic Truth
Society in 1900, he argued the case for a modern
university linked to "industrial pursuits":

"The people do not know, and cannot know,
the countless ways in which their exclusion from
higher education works into the social system and
lowers the entire tone of existence, and weakens its
powers and practically paralyzes it."

Tompkins underlined this passage.

The Danish Folk School movement also attracted Tompkins' attention. Founded by Bishop
Nikolai Grundtvig (1783-1872), a Lutheran theolo-

gian, poet, and the spiritual father of democracy in Denmark, this unique system of adult education had made many of the people of that country efficient, competitive, and spiritually strong. Grundtvig devoted his life to moving Denmark from medievalism to modernity, striving to create a "school of life" based on "the living word," not on dry, scholastic learning. He had deep faith in the wisdom of the ordinary people, believed in the possibilities of "Life's Enlightenment" based on lived experience and the language arising from it. Grundtvig saw the need for a new type of school which would bring people to life, encourage them to see, to think, to use their powers.

Grundtvig's visionary spirit for his people fused with that of Tompkins for eastern Nova Scotians. Tompkins wrote: "The ABC of democracy is that the brains of the world should be organized and mobilized. This surely is fitting work for the Christian men and women."

TOMPKINS DECIDED that a dramatic move was needed, an action that would shake up the church and the university, disturb their complacency, and make their people think!

In 1921, with the bravado of a Martin Luther challenging the established thinking of church and campus, Tompkins decided to nail his theses to the wall of the Diocese of Antigonish. The fiery priest took a sabbatical, put his ideas about education to paper, and issued *Knowledge for the People: A Call to St. Francis Xavier College.* He printed and distributed 5,000 copies of this short, thirty-one page pamphlet, said to have been paid for by Neil McNeil of Boston.

Knowledge for the People began by noting that the desire of people "for more Knowledge, better intellectual training, and better organized effort in their various callings" had gripped men and women everywhere "without regard to condition, class or circumstances." It continued:

"Men and women everywhere are clamoring for the equal opportunity that education and intellectual training [can give].... There have not been two types of V.C.'s [Victoria Crosses] nor two types of wooden crosses in the Flanders field." Ordinary people had suffered during the war "and now that peace has come they seek an equal share of opportunity and in the good and worth while things in life."

During the war, "educational extension" had been used to tell people about the policies of the Allies and of their enemies. In 1917, the Canadian YMCA and the chaplain service of the Canadian Army set up Khaki College under the direction of Dr. Henry Marshall Tory, president of the University of Alberta and a pioneer in taking knowledge to the people. About fifty thousand learners studied in nineteen centres to prepare themselves for demobilization and return to civilian life.

In *Knowledge for the People*, Tompkins listed the "considerations" that made "the present time a fertile field for Educational Extension": returned soldiers newly aware of the importance of education who could not go to college; increases in wages, better prices for products, shorter hours; the removal of temptation to dissipation with the introduction of prohibition; farmers' and workers' movements; the granting of the franchise to women; and the "considerable number of boys and girls from 16 to 25 years who...have received little intellectual training" but who would take advantage of it if it were available.

The pamphlet reviewed and praised the activities of the Workers' Educational Association, the Gaelic League in Ireland, the University of Wisconsin, and ventures in adult education in Quebec and Saskatchewan. Tompkins made tart references to the University of Toronto where people sought "a shaking up of the dry bones among the staff." He lamented the lack of qualified teachers in rural Nova Scotia, a situation inhibiting local development.

During diocesan meetings between 1918 and 1921, discussions had focused on what could be done to revitalize life in a land where rural decline had begun to accelerate. *Knowledge for the People* promoted consolidated high schools, good roads, modern farming, health promotion and improved education. Tompkins claimed that Nova Scotia was "pregnant with sympathy for improvement of the education system." Then he sounded a prophetic note in language reminiscent of the Bible:

"It is a law that popular governments and popular institutions, whether religious or secular, are

**Three photographs of
Father James John Tompkins**

Father Moses Coady
The first Director of the
St. Francis Xavier University
Extension Department, 1930-52

The Saint Francis Xavier University Years

Rev. Dr. Hugh MacPherson
"Little Doc Hugh"

Rev. Dr. Hugh P. MacPherson
"The Old Rector"
Rector, St. F.X., 1906-1936

Neil McNeil, "The Builder," and Dr. John Somers
Father Jimmy: "I cultivated them for a long time." Father Jimmy once explained
that he dug ditches and waited for someone with means to fall into them!

The first People's School, 1921
Priests at centre front: Fathers Jimmy Tompkins and Moses Coady

Bishop James Morrison
Diocese of Antigonish
1912-1950

Father Michael Gillis
Father Coady called him
"the creative mind
behind all movements,
the dynamic leader and inspirer"

Another photograph of the first People's School, 1921

The Canso Years

John Chafe

Mother M. Faustina MacArthur
of the Sisters of Saint Martha

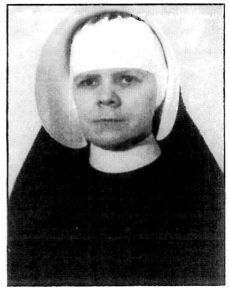

Sister Mary Concepta Fougere
Sisters of Saint Martha

Sister Denis Marie Mulcahy
Sisters of Saint Martha

The first three sisters to answer Father Jimmy's call
for help in Canso. Photos courtesy of the congregation
of the Sisters of Saint Martha Archives.

Left:
Mary Arnold (at right in the photo) with the study group working with models of houses that they planned to build

Above:
The Arnold Housing Club buying the land for Tompkinsville, March, 1938

Right:
Father Jimmy with Sister Francis Dolores in the library at Reserve Mines

Co-operative Store Board of Directors, Reserve Mines
Front row, left to right: Jimmy Marsh, Rod Campbell, Charlie Currie,
Don McQueen (manager), Mickie Currie. Back row: Joe Laben,
Bernie Borden, unidentified, unidentified, Carrigan.

**Right:
Father Jimmy
Tompkins with
George and Jean
Clarke and son,
Saunder, in front
of their house in
Tompkinsville.**

Father Jimmy

**Left:
Joe & Mary Laben
Cooperative Housing
Pioneers, in their home in
Tompkinsville, 1977**

**Right:
Judy Laidlaw-Hines works on a
bust of Father Jimmy Tompkins,
created with the help of her instructor, Mother Sister Philip,
circa 1953**

subject to decay if they lose touch with the people. They may even become tyrannous if they fall into the hands of men immune to accountability, either because the people, whom they are supposed to represent and serve, have lost the will or the power to hold them to account. They are subject to decay also if they fail to adjust themselves to the changing needs of the times. In their decadence they not infrequently become the tool of a clique or class maintaining the semblance of life rather than the reality. These facts are painted large on the map of the world. Institutions for the whole people are not self-perpetuating machines set once for all in perpetual motion. They are living organisms whose roots are in the people, and unless they draw from these roots, the material of life, the tree will die, will be cut down and burnt."

Tompkins insisted that the university should take useful information to those outside its walls. St. F.X. had the resources, and a modest beginning could be made by calling a conference of educators and people from agriculture and industry: "'We are at your service,' our educators must say. 'Tell us how best we can serve you.'" A new kind of priest, like Little Doc Hugh, St. F.X.'s pioneering agricultural field worker, could serve as extension workers among rural people.

"We need a handful of devoted men prepared to make this work their single interest, and to consecrate to it their whole time and energies for no compensation beyond daily bread if necessary.

And just because their work, so arduous, so exacting, (and full, it may be, of disappointment and discouragement), must be its own reward, these men cannot normally be drawn from the laity. We eagerly court the cooperation of the laity in this undertaking, but the sacrifices which our principal workers must make are greater than we may reasonably expect from the average layman."

Here was a New Testament vision of the role of the priest, as Tompkins recalled how thousands of Canadians had died in foreign fields, and others returned maimed from the war "as the consequence of taking a stand for the right." The cadre of "priest teachers" he envisaged would educate local people through "corporeal charity" and would recruit lay people to work for the "establishment of a kingdom of God upon earth."

In the fall of 1920, Tompkins explained to Rev. Thomas Shahan: "We have in mind the setting up of an organization for reaching the people that may be fraught with wonderful possibilities. You can hardly imagine what a change has come over the outlook of people all through this country within the last few years."

IN JANUARY, 1921, the first People's School opened on the St. F.X. campus. A photograph of those taking part in this pioneering venture shows a group of men clad in sombre suits and ties, a few wearing sweaters, all looking very serious. Father Jimmy sits in the front row, looking serene, while

44

next to him Father Coady lifts his eyes heaven-wards. The participants in the experiment in adult education had been recruited through ads in *The Casket* and other newspapers and through informal contacts with parish priests. The ages of the fifty-one participants—which included only one woman—ranged from seventeen to fifty-seven, and they studied Arithmetic, English, Economics, Chemistry, Physics, Business, Finance, Public Speaking, Agriculture, Stock Breeding, Veterinary Hygiene, Biology and Natural Resources. No tests for entry into the school were required, nor was a fee charged. Holding the event between January and March meant that men would be available, free of the demands made by their work in agriculture and the fisheries.

In May, 1921, a brochure described the purpose and the history of the People's School—and "What the Professors, the Students, and the Public say about it." Its cover noted that the provincial Department of Agriculture "tangibly expressed its interest in and approbation of the People's School by making a substantial contribution" to its expenses and also by covering the cost of the pamphlet. The foreword by Bishop Morrison congratulated St. F.X. for "bringing knowledge to the people through this un-tried channel." He echoed one of Father Jimmy's themes when he added: "It can be said that it was nothing less than a revelation to observe what an amount of latent intellectual talent has been lying around undeveloped, and thereby precluded from attaining its proper destiny both as to individual needs and for the country's best welfare."

Three epigrams on a separate page precede an introduction by Father Jimmy on "The 'Highway' versus the 'Ladder.'" One encapsulates his philosophy of education: "We are more interested in and concerned with the education of the masses than with the polishing of culture for a few." Tompkins points out the reason for launching the People's School: "It is the desire to help develop the submerged 70 to 80 per cent of our population...." He added that "a recent pamphlet entitled 'Knowledge for the People,' which may be had from the secretary of the People's School, Antigonish, for the asking" had shown how successful the Workers' Educational Association had been in bringing knowledge to the common people of England:

"In a smaller way the record of the students of our People's School is another proof that the grown-up man of little or no previous education is capable of remarkable development if he possesses ambition and average intelligence."

Tompkins then cites a study of three million soldiers by the United States War Department's Division of Civil Training that indicated that "only 10 per cent of the best brains of the country are college bred."

The eleven instructors at the school—who included the principal of the Truro Agricultural College, a manager of the Canadian Bank of Commerce, Fathers Miles Tompkins, Moses Coady, and Little

Doc Hugh—set down their impressions of their experiences with enthusiasm and suggested that this approach to adult education should continue. Sixteen students added their comments, including:

L. Timmons, miner, age 23, New Waterford, C.B., (Left school in 6th grade): "It is a thing that the working people, especially those in Cape Breton, have long been waiting for. It is a return to the people for the effort they have made to help the college. It is an awakening to the fact, that, in this age of science and atheism, education of the laymen is necessary to solidify and promote the position of Christianity in this world."

J.L. MacPherson, railwayman, age 26, Whitney Pier, C.B. (Left school in 5th grade): "I feel that this course of only two months has enlivened in me a longing for more knowledge and education...."

H.F. MacDonald, a farmer, always hated farming, but the professors showed him that it was "as big a profession as any and anyone coming from the farm need not be ashamed of it." S.K. MacKinnon, another farmer, wrote about how the course "Opened our minds to new lines of thought and study we never dreamed of before." He added: "The recent Great War has demonstrated that one man is about as good as another as far as native ability is concerned. This has caused a great wave of democracy to spread over the country."

A section headed "Tributes from the Public," praises the school and *Knowledge for the People*. The Municipal Council of the County of Antigonish passed a resolution endorsing the People's School, and "A Word of Appreciation from Québec" with no name attached, stated:

"You have hit upon—designedly I know—what must be the initial movement in any 'social action' which wishes to have any appreciable and permanent effect—the forming of an elite among the people, a wide awake advance guard of men who know how, and therefore are willing to help themselves."

Dr. J.A. Bancroft, Dawson, Professor of Geology at McGill University, hoped "your flame becomes a veritable conflagration." An editorial in the *Morning Chronicle* of April 23, 1921, stated: "This is the most notable experience in university extension work which has been undertaken in Canada, as far as we know...." An editorial in *The United Farmers' Guide* also lavished praise on the venture, as did the secretary of the National Council of Education in Winnipeg.

THE SMALL BAND of learners had been treated like important people in Antigonish, welcomed by the mayor and some of the university faculty. They recognized that their presence at St. F.X. represented something very new. And they responded enthusiastically to this educational challenge. Tompkins wrote: "It is a perfect joy to see the avidity with which these men are striving after knowledge." To his friend Neil McNeil, the priest noted the "perfect delight and wonder to see them work." He added that Stephen John MacKinnon, who later became a university extension worker, "leads off as number one. He is swallowing things like an Indian juggler."

It looked to Tompkins as if his cause for adult education for the common people had finally triumphed. The *Halifax Herald* of May 28, 1921, two months after the People's School ended, claimed:

"For many years universities have been, and most of them are, labouring under the misconception that they by divine right, shall serve the wealthy and privileged classes, and in no degree popular education."

The next People's School, held in 1922, attracted sixty participants, and its future seemed assured. Several of those who attended the first one had suggested the need for the university to take knowledge to the people through extension courses. The very enthusiasm for actually bringing ordinary people to the campus may well have blunted efforts to do this.

AND FATHER TOMPKINS, perhaps believing that he had won one battle, turned his attention to another—the cause of university amalgamation in Atlantic Canada proposed by the Carnegie Corporation. But the little priest polarized people.

"You loved him—or you hated him." "He did not have an easy disposition." "He constantly challenged the established order whenever it became a stumbling block to progress. He never knew the meaning of fear."

Even those who warmed their hands at his fire found a way of avoiding action.

"Perhaps he talked too much and too vehemently. Perhaps his challenge to the educators caused vague comfort in the minds of those who also saw what was happening but believed that someone other than the educators should accept the responsibility of bringing in reform."

Father Jimmy continued to support the Carnegie Corporation's proposal to merge the region's universities with his usual energy, enthusiasm and optimism, serving as the local champion of the idea.

The corporation set up a commission in May 1921 to survey the educational scene in Atlantic Canada. A two-man commission—made up of W.S. Learned of the corporation and K.C.W. Sills, the Nova Scotia-born president of Bowdoin College, Maine—looked at ways of bringing higher education in Atlantic Canada up to the standards prevailing elsewhere in North America. Their report, *Education in the Maritime Provinces*, appeared in 1922, and showed great sensitivity to the lifestyle in the region, describing it as "a conservative, chiefly small-town rural life...thoroughly denominationalized." It identified the weaknesses of higher education as underfunding, inadequate facilities and fragmented effort.

The report described St. F.X. as a "very genuine institution" with strong links to its constituency through its teacher training program for rural areas and its People's School. Unified educational effort and a higher standard of academic excellence, however, required a central university.

Father Jimmy supported the idea of university amalgamation long before the Learned-Sills report appeared. On July 30, 1922, he wrote to Angus L. Macdonald, then a Halifax lawyer and newspaper publisher who became premier of Nova Scotia in 1933:

"Get your coat off in good earnest. We have the best case in the world and no better cause was ever placed before the people of these provinces.... We *ought* to win and it will be *our own fault* if we don't. Failure will spell disaster for us all. Success will bring a new and glorious era to these provinces and give our poor people a chance for life in these strenuous days."

The merger idea received support in some academic circles, especially since the Carnegie Corporation offered three million dollars to achieve it. It was argued that one large university, rather than many scattered small ones, would have the resources to prepare young people to develop themselves, their region and their country.

Tompkins was also concerned that a federation of universities *without* St. Francis Xavier would draw the best teachers, further isolating St. F.X. and poor Catholic students, and keeping St. F.X. from being a respected institution on its own.

But opposition to the amalgamation began to surface throughout 1922, with Bishop Morrison leading the charge. He had supported the idea of the People's School because it suited his essentially rural views of what constituted the good life. Cautious, conservative, and moderate, the bishop feared the urbanizing and commercializing thrusts emerging in eastern Nova Scotia as society there moved from a subsistence to a market economy. If St. F.X. sent its students to Halifax, they were bound to become secularized. Federation looked to him and many others like a step toward a "semi-catholic, semi-pagan education, an education that will result in fewer men for the priesthood." The bishop found a ready ally in Dr. Hugh MacPherson, "The Old Rector," president of St. F.X., who stated bluntly: "Personally, I dread this scheme." These two men determined to stop the merger, and focused on its main proponent—Father Jimmy.

IN 1922, St. F.X. UNIVERSITY HAD 245 students and faculty, and served as a stable point of reference in the lives of everyone in Antigonish and the diocese. During his twenty-year tenure at the university, Father Jimmy had made significant contributions to its growth and development. He had raised funds, encouraged talent wherever he found it, and fostered a vision of how the university could serve the ordinary people. Unlike Bishop Morrison, who had concerns about working with Protestants, the fiery priest cared not a jot for denominational differences and did not think Catholicism would be endangered by amalgamation.

In January, 1922, the St. F.X. faculty, prodded by Father Jimmy, passed a unanimous resolution supporting amalgamation. He had articles printed in *The Casket*, hailing the Carnegie scheme as the solution to the problems of education in the Maritimes. He encouraged the United Mine Workers in Cape Breton to start their own college as part of the new consortium of universities.

The summer of 1922 saw many meetings and discussions about amalgamation, dividing clergy and students and faculty. On August 1, the Board of Governors at St. F.X. set up a committee to study the merger, and Bishop Morrison referred the matter to the Vatican for the Pope's decision.

The undated report submitted to the Board of Governors threw up a barrage of objections to the proposed federation, quoting authorities as diverse as a "writer in the *Dublin Review*, Dec. 1851, p. 585" and Thorstein Veblen "by many considered the most brilliant mind in America." The report had two consistent arguments, two overwhelming fears about a merger—the belief that St. F.X. would lose control over its own destiny and that young Catholics would abandon their faith:

"The troubles of the world today are due to the divorce of religion and education.... The remedy lies not in less religion in college and university teaching, but more."

At a secular university, young Catholics would have no access to Christian teachings, whereas, under the present system "graduates shall be strong to serve, and powerful enough to battle the evil of the world, and construct virtue in the characters of men and women."

The core of the brief emerged in the following passage:

"Going into the merger would mean practically giving up of control of Catholic College education.... The social welfare of the country demands that our main source of right principles and of Christian leaders be kept intact and allowed to do its work freely."

The report noted the low salaries of faculty, and the lack of books at St. F.X., but stressed that it could be run as an efficient college. In no way would it be able to sustain its identity and mandate if it became part of a semi-pagan, materialistic, non-sectarian, relativistic conglomeration.

WHEN THE VATICAN responded to Bishop Morrison's request, it came out against amalgamation. Father Jimmy responded to this in his characteristic way: "We know more about our business than Rome does."

But even before Rome spoke, Bishop Morrison had decided to deal with his troublesome priest—"the prime mover among Catholics [for the] deadly proposition"—by transferring him off the campus. In early December, Father Jimmy was told to go to Canso as parish priest.

When told of his fate, Tompkins went to see his cousin. Trembling as he spoke, he asked Coady,

"What if I do not go? What if I go away from here entirely? They're looking for priests." Coady had little to offer. He is said to have replied simply, "Go to Canso. Go, and obey your bishop. Go."

In May, Tompkins had written to Dr. William Learned at the Carnegie Corporation: "The powers of darkness and reaction have been making a dead set upon us and I am the bad man."

CHAPTER THREE

The Wilderness Prophet

"I have a good reason to believe that my exile...gives the movement quite an impetus."

Father Jimmy Tompkins

MYTHOLOGIES CLING LIKE SEA FOG to Father Jimmy's twelve-year sojourn in Canso.

On a summer's day, the town looked like an archetypal Nova Scotian fishing village. In the time of the priest's arrival, winter travellers from Antigonish took the train to Mulgrave, and then a three-hour boat ride along the coast to reach the community. Boats also connected Canso with villages along the Eastern Shore and Halifax. In summer, a bus bumped along rough roads to Antigonish.

An early report stated, "Canceau is one of the best places for codfishing.... There are several fine beaches to dry fish on and several small islands where ships can be sheltered." The name derives from the Micmac *Kamsok*—"the place beyond the cliffs." In 1606, French settlers from Port Royal moved here to join others who had arrived two years earlier. Few people wintered over at Canso. The rough shelters and crude fort here were destroyed several times during the struggle between the French and English that marked the century and a half after the first settlement.

Lying on Chedabucto Bay, at the extreme southeastern tip of mainland Nova Scotia, the site of Canso offered excellent access to rich offshore fishing grounds. But it only became a permanent settlement in 1812. The surrounding seas were rich in fish, but the land offered little to sustain life. Grey-brown rock dominates the town, built on a series of barren hills rising from the sea. Southwest of the town lies Dover (now called Little Dover), an even rockier and more barren place. Few trees grow along this coast, and those that do are wind-bent away from the sea.

THE IMPRESSION IS OFTEN GIVEN that Father Jimmy arrived in a depressed, benighted community of poor fisherfolk, and immediately organized the local people to take charge of their own destinies. The real story is much more complex, much more radical than this legend.

Father Jimmy's parish extended along the Canso coast, stretching about thirty kilometres and including the town of Canso, the village of Dover, and the hamlet of Queensport. He travelled with the mail run to the small communities, often being stormstayed during the winter. It took the wilderness prophet four and a half years of hard, steady persuasion before the defining moment came that offered a focus for the discontent among the fishermen and moved them into collective action.

Father Jimmy came to Canso at a critical time in the community's history. Throughout the nineteenth century, Canso offered a prosperous living for some people. The large houses of the fish merchants still dot the community. Between 1881 and 1894, transatlantic cables operated by two companies landed here. The employees of Western Union Cable Company lived in well-built houses on the company's own street. Those of Commercial Cable occupied a row of houses on Hazel Hill. The town, sure of its destiny, had incorporated in 1901 and seemed to have an assured future as a major communications link between North America and Europe. But in that same year, Marconi received the world's first wireless transatlantic radio transmission at Signal Hill in Newfoundland. This new technology would render communication by cable obsolete.

By 1922, the community had a wide range of facilities and services, including several wharves, four fish plants, a cold storage facility, post office, the two cable stations, and a theatre. Good houses flanked the main street. The most powerful man in town, H.F. Robinson, hailed from Gloucester, Massachusetts, and worked for the Montreal-based Maritime Fish Corporation whose sign dominated the waterfront. It owned Canso Cold Storage, did a million dollars' worth of business a year, and paid only $3,000 annually in taxes. Robinson practised journalism, served as spokesman for his company and as secretary of the Board of Trade. He had also been mayor of Canso. The first mayor, who served from 1901 to 1911, belonged to the Whitman family, another group of fish barons who played a leading role in the community. Leaders of such organizations as the Imperial Order of the Daughters of the Empire were wives of the local business aristocracy.

In 1928, the town and the Board of Trade issued a 63-page booklet to mark the unveiling of the Canso Cairn, an historical marker, on July 2. The photographs show prosperous-looking businessmen, well dressed, solemn looking, clad in three-piece suits with watch chains over their paunches. The booklet contains no shots of the men who worked on the fishing boats or the women who processed the catches. These people had been pushed to the edges of the community. According to a newspaper report in 1927, their houses were "mere shelters" containing nothing of "beauty or brightness."

In the following year, Father Jimmy, astonished that his coal bill was $708.27, lamented:

"Is it any wonder that many around these shores live on bread and molasses and live in houses sheathed with wallpaper?"

The spire of the Star of the Sea Church dominated the community, rising above a scatter of wooden houses called "Irish Town." Opened in

September, 1891, its gothic architecture, snowy white walls, high pillars crowned with artistic capitols, and arched vault symbolized the good times in the community and the confidence of the days of its construction.

FATHER JIMMY ARRIVED IN CANSO knowing little about parish life, of the round of masses, confessions, visits, baptisms, funerals that made up priestly work. At St. F.X., where he was surrounded by a corps of dedicated followers, the priest had concentrated on the big picture, conjuring up visions of Nova Scotia's future where education and development would go hand in hand. Now he had to confront the day-to-day problems of survival in a small fishing community.

William Learned, his friend at the Carnegie Corporation, had written to Father Jimmy before his departure from Antigonish:

"I feel very certain that your sojourn in the desert will be brief, since the pressure of public opinion cannot fail to react vigorously to such ill-judged and arbitrary action."

But Father Jimmy remained in the "desert" for the rest of his life.

Father Coady wrote of his cousin that he had "boundless faith in the ordinary man." Leo MacIntyre, another of his followers, called him a "true religious reformer motivated by a love which excluded no one, not even those who opposed his ideas.... He was a man ahead of his time but in another sense he was a primitive Christian...."

But what could he do for his poverty-stricken parishioners, perpetually in debt to the merchants who bought their fish? What could he do with the men and women who appeared to have no ambition to improve their lot? What could he do with the majority of Canso residents eking out a bare living, and prey to lethargy, lassitude and despair? What could he do about poor nutrition that deformed the legs of children?

And what could he do about the rectory?

The big, drafty building had an uncertain heating system, and the roof leaked from time to time. A man might be "blown off his feet in a corridor" when the wind set in from the sea. These winds also drove damp, clammy air into the rectory through any and every opening. "It's so damp here a man feels waterlogged."

In April, 1923, Father Jimmy lay shivering in bed, wearing an overcoat. At least in this cold room, this side of the house, he could escape the noisy foghorn that made the other bedroom uninhabitable, and which had nearly driven him mad.

Then a visitor arrived.

And Father Jimmy met his most valuable ally in the community. Described as "tall and distinguished," John Chafe, a Western Union cable company official, would later call his friend "the most unforgettable character I ever met" in an article for *Reader's Digest*. Chafe, a Newfoundlander, was a practical man with secure employment, standing in the community, a good house, and a car. He was in no way beholden to the fish barons who dominated life in Canso. The man Chafe saw in bed looked sick and lonely, coughing away, surrounded by papers, pamphlets and books, complaining, "Can't get warm here."

Chafe handed the priest a warm letter of introduction from Archbishop Roche of Newfoundland, who had learned of Father Jimmy's exile and sent Chafe to comfort him. The priest called the archbishop a "good man," then pointed out that the light in the room was not working properly. Chafe fixed it. Father Jimmy told the visitor of his discontents.

The Newfoundlander cut him short, asking, "Is there a hot water bottle in the house?" Removing the clutter from the bed—and the coat from the man in it—Chafe gave Father Jimmy his medicine.

Their friendship blossomed. Father Jimmy would phone Chafe most evenings and ask him what he was doing. They would travel the rough roads in Chafe's car, with Father Jimmy pointing out the miserable shacks in which the fishermen and their families lived. To assuage his anger, the two men would say the rosary.

At St. F.X. Father Jimmy had espoused education in abstract terms. Now he had to examine exactly what kind of education ordinary people needed to solve their own problems.

ECONOMIC DECLINE ACCELERATED in the Maritimes as Father Jimmy took up his unaccustomed role of parish priest. The World War had disrupted established trade patterns. Newfoundland fish merchants lost markets in Europe and began to compete in those in which Nova Scotia sold its catches, including the Caribbean.

Factories in Ontario and Quebec had expanded during the war, and now produced more goods than their home markets could absorb. Shifting their operations to making needed items for peacetime, Upper Canadian companies exported their products to the Maritimes, undercutting businesses there. They bought up local factories, and the Maritimes became a branch plant economy. The tariff system favoured manufacturers in Central Canada and imposed heavy charges on imports that would compete with what they produced, so people in the Maritimes could not obtain even necessities at lower rates from the United States.

As the Depression deepened, factories shut down or went on short time. Between 1920 and '26, 42% of the manufacturing jobs in the region simply vanished. The steel mills and coal mines in Cape Breton put their workers on reduced work weeks and cut their pay. In 1925, coal miners went on strike, looting and burning down company stores.

The federal and provincial governments appeared paralyzed and powerless in the face of economic decline. The grip of outside interests on the Maritimes tightened through the decade, as financiers in Toronto and Montreal slowly took over banking institutions and consolidated them. Most Maritimers had no access to banking and saving services that would keep money in their communities and serve local needs. Freight rates rose, making regional exports less competitive in Canadian markets. Nova Scotia had entered Confederation in 1867 as an equal partner with other founding provinces. Now, as population increased in Upper Canada and the West, the Maritime Provinces had fewer and fewer seats in the House of Commons, less and less power in Ottawa, and a declining ability to protect and forward the interests of those who lived in the region.

Tompkins understood what was happening in his part of the world:

"The injury done to [the Maritime Provinces] by the absence of banking institutions, controlled within the provinces and by our own people, is far-reaching and irreparable. Large enterprises—and these are the days of large enterprise—are not launched on fifty or five thousand dollars.... Any large accommodation must naturally come through Montreal or Toronto, through the dozen men who control the money of Canada, men whose financial eyes may be scanning the possibilities of big and quick returns in South America or Siberia and thinking little about the fishermen, miners or farmers of Nova Scotia. At best they might be induced to advance money to firms in Montreal or Toronto who do business with them, for the purpose of carrying on branches of the same businesses in these provinces. And thus the control of our industries moves west—so do the profits. Maritimers do the servile work and profit accordingly."

Father Jimmy could attack the "Cream Skimmers," monopolizers, industrial and financial despots. But how would this help poor fisherfolk to make a better life for themselves and their children?

ALTHOUGH BY NATURE impatient and aggressive, the little priest did not rush into solving the community problems of poor fisherfolk. Instead, he acted as an animator. He knew the right questions to ask about the misery and ignorance he saw all around him—and pointed listeners to sources where they could find answers. Sitting on a pickle barrel in a country store, cigar stub held in place with a toothpick, Father Jimmy listened to fishermen complain about the price of fish and the cost of supplies.

"What problems do you think are worst?" he would ask.

His friend John Chafe, a man with a passion for community development, reported:

"He kept needling the fishermen. 'Why do you get only a cent and a half for cod when it's sold in Halifax for thirty?' he'd ask. Or, 'How come you sell your lobsters for seven cents when hotels charge a dollar? Some smart son-of-a-gun's making a lot out of your hard work, eh?' When he'd upset enough fishermen with his questions, Father Jimmy herded them into small study groups."

Father Jimmy wrote: "I notice in Canso, for instance—an important fishing centre—that the people are poorer and more dependent today than they were twenty years ago. They damn the place, their employment and their employers. They do not know what the matter is, and they are too poor and ignorant to find out for themselves. The reason back of it all is that they are being exploited by fish firms owned by men in Montreal and anywhere else except Canso....

"And so we become a branch people, and a few places hundreds and thousands of miles away skim off the cream, which goes into the pockets of a very few—not the best place to keep cream, but you will forgive the figure."

Tompkins urged the fishermen to think about their plight—and the reasons for it. He'd hand out a book, clipping, pamphlet to anyone and everyone: "Read this and you'll learn something." Then he'd urge listeners: "Learn all you can and share what you learn."

He had no illusions about how people lived in fishing communities. Urban mythologies portrayed fisherfolk as honest, hard-working people living simple, decent lives while wresting a living from the cruel sea. Those marketing tourism painted a picture of archetypal Maritimers dwelling in quaint, peaceful villages, imbued with virtues lacking in city dwellers.

Tompkins knew that fishing families struggled hard to survive. In the off-seasons, fishermen and others provided a ready body of cheap labour for public works. The prevailing system of pork-barrel, pothole politics ensured that if they voted the right way they would be able to earn a few dollars fixing the roads. To pick up a little cash, wives worked in fish plants at low wages. Small gardens, nourished by seaweed, grew vegetables. Families combed the barrens behind the town for blueberries and anything edible.

Some local people in Canso trapped mink and sold the pelts. Father Jimmy sought advice about starting mink farms, but nothing came of this initiative. He proposed setting up a university department at St. F.X. to study the problems of the fisheries and a research centre at Canso for the same purpose. His mind twisted and turned, forever seeking ways to solve problems, to enlighten the people, to accelerate learning processes.

The small priest had a powerful presence, although he was "no thundering spellbinder," as a friend put it. He scattered around ideas, inspired others, made people think. As Moses Coady wrote:

"Dr. Tompkins' greatness is of the kind that defies classification by all ordinary rules; in this, in itself, is the greatest tribute we can pay him. He was a personality of many facets."

Nothing moved him as much as poverty or angered him more than ignorance. In his parish, Father Jimmy would "scurry around all day, minding everyone's business at the top of his voice." He brought engineers, judges, politicians, and others to his parish to give talks. In Dover, he rounded up the local youth in Ed Boudreau's store. He found someone to teach them to read, then sat at the door so no one could escape.

DOVER LAY eight kilometres from Canso, and life in the small community of four hundred people had a desperate edge to it. His first sermon to his parishioners here must have surprised them. He read from the Gospel of the day, then closed his Bible with a thump. Then he announced:

"I'm not going to talk to you on the Gospel of the day. There is another matter. I've been told that some of you take things one from another. I understand that some do not get enough to eat for themselves or their families and take it where they can find it. I'm not going to say anything about that either."

The priest had learned of local thefts of fishing nets, boots, pieces of pork. He hated the sins—but not the sinners. Father Jimmy wanted to know why people stole from each other. To keep body and soul together? To keep husband and wife and family in the same miserable shack? Surely there was enough work in the community and enough fish in the sea to satisfy the needs of everyone!

The people of Dover sensed they had an ally in their ongoing struggle to survive, as Father Jimmy announced that he was throwing in his lot with theirs:

"Even Christ did not undertake to preach to

men who were hungry."

Parishioners found the priest less interested in their sins than in their progress. As his presence became felt in the small community, non-Catholics often came to Mass to hear Father Jimmy. He'd follow Mass in Latin with readings in English by his assistants. He knew that charity offered only temporary relief for the poor, that grand schemes to improve their lot needed time to plan and implement.

"If the government gives a man a $10 dole, he needs another as soon as it's gone. And he hasn't learned a damn thing, except how to stick out his hand." But, he pointed out, "When a man gets up on his hind legs, no one can walk for him."

Father Jimmy moved around his parish, pockets crammed with pamphlets and clippings, urging those who listened to him to learn about what was happening to them. He met with the Holy Name Society, giving out readings, forever asking questions, poking and prodding away at the sources of local discontent. He invited experts to come up with answers to the problems of poverty.

J.C.F. MacDonnell, an agricultural representative who always carried a little booklet, *Who Owns Canada*, answered his call and came to Dover to examine the prospects for raising goats. The community had one cow and scores of malnourished children. Father Jimmy took the ag. rep. (agricultural representative) into the homes of the poor. What was this woman feeding her children? "Loaf bread and water," she replied.

"Pick up that child," the priest ordered Mac-Donnell. When the visitor did so, he learned about the meaning of poverty.

As they returned to Canso, the two men spotted a road gang. "Sound your horn, and stop the car," Father Jimmy ordered. Twenty men gathered and the priest introduced the stranger. Pointing to a large rock, he asked MacDonnell to mount it and talk about the care, feeding and management of goats. The ag. rep. really did not know much about goats, but did his best. When local people heard a horn, Father Jimmy told MacDonnell as they returned to the car, they knew "they were wanted for something."

Shortly after the visit, MacDonnell received a telegram from the priest:

"Excellent people. Hot foot after goats. Send them along."

The Department of Agriculture obtained the animals from British Columbia and followed Father Jimmy's directions. When the goats arrived, no one in the community knew how to care for them—despite MacDonnell's lecture. The animals adapted to the local environment and thrived, living off the land, and giving milk that greatly improved the local diet. This incident illustrates Father Jimmy's style. Once he found a solution to a problem, he called in an expert to tell the local people about it, secured the resources to implement it, and then left things to unfold. (A woman in Dover praised the goat's milk and offered Father Jimmy a glass of it.

He drank it down and felt very queasy.)

FISHERMEN IN CANSO and elsewhere in the region worked in highly individualistic and competitive ways. They fished the inshore waters from small boats that they owned. Brothers, sons, other relatives helped out with the fishing. You did not need a great deal of capital to go into fishing. Fish landed at the dock were examined by commission merchants who offered a price. The merchants had no particular interest in competing with each other. If a stubborn fisherman held out for a higher price than was offered for his catch, then it could rot where it lay. If he had an account with a merchant who had supplied him with equipment, then his catch—at whatever price the supplier chose to pay—went to reduce the debt.

The Canso fishermen had a union, but it was moribund, powerless. Many of the fishermen were illiterate, and Father Jimmy had to help them to read before they could make use of the printed information he dispensed. The priest recognized where the main problem of securing a better life for fishermen lay:

"The field of marketing gives men a chance to come together, helps to eliminate exploitation, produces quality goods, saves the consumer, etc. With the money that is gathered together from the sale of consumer goods and with the credit unions, the people are in a position to engage in larger things— in industry and production, in wholesaling...."

"The fall of the Roman Empire began with the capture of the outposts. So must the first round of our victory be won in the rural districts. Cut off, by cooperation, the rivulets that flow from the country to the city magnates and that impoverish correspondingly rural population, and you have won your first victory.... Capture the country for cooperation, and puncture the balloons of the city airdwellers, and we shall all get back to earth in a little time."

Ordinary people needed education rooted in their lives, *adult* education combining spiritual and practical works of mercy. Through it, they would learn to feed themselves, build better houses, meet their needs and those of others more effectively—and live better lives. Father Jimmy saw cooperatives as places where the needs of people took precedence over profits. But he knew that little could be done in places like Canso and Dover if capital was lacking. While in debt to merchants or forced to take any asking price for their catches, local fishermen could never save enough money to expand or improve their operations.

And in the 1920s, a new threat appeared to the livelihoods of the small boat fishermen and those who worked for the large companies. The corporate giants working the Atlantic acquired large beam trawlers. These large, crewed ships, which had appeared in Nova Scotian waters as early as 1908, were seen as a more efficient and profitable way to harvest the sea. The Maritime Fish Corporation based its huge trawler, *Rayon d'Or*, at Canso. *The Canso Breeze and Guysboro County Advocate* described it as "undoubtedly a great benefit to the community."

Such vessels required fewer and more skilled workers to catch more fish. Foreign trawlers began to work the offshore waters. The federal government banned the use of steam trawlers within five kilometres of the coast, the limit of the country's territorial waters, in 1908. And so the inshore fishery survived. But the economics of fishing were against it. Nova Scotia had a schooner fishery, and it too was under threat from trawlers. A schooner with twenty-four men took two weeks to fill its small holds with the cod the men in its dories caught with their handlines. Beam trawlers scooped everything up in their nets, and in five days caught an average of eighty thousand kilos of fish.

In 1912, the responsible minister claimed that "effective steps will be taken" to prevent trawlers from taking over the industry. But it was an empty promise. By the end of World War One the trawler fleets had grown.

Year after year, Father Jimmy kept barraging people with information and ideas, forever reading, talking, writing letters to a wide range of correspondents, keeping in touch with trends in the outside world and with what was happening in the diocese. A visiting journalist discovered that Father Jimmy had turned the front room of the glebe house into a reading room. Newspaper racks held *The New York Times* and its weekly edition. Three or four fishermen entered the room. Father Jimmy told one of them to pick up the last issue of the *Times*, and read out a piece about workers' cooperative housing in Vienna.

AND TOMPKINS TRAVELLED.

In June, 1924, he went to New York to attend a meeting called by the Carnegie Corporation to discuss adult education—the only Canadian invited to participate. Here he pointed out the need to combat illiteracy. From this gathering came the American Association for Adult Education, formed in 1926. Father Jimmy served as one of its inner circle for the next twenty years. His fame began to spread, and in his early years in Canso he received an invitation from a progressive bishop in Oklahoma to work in that state. But he stayed in Canso.

The impressions of those who knew Father Jimmy reveal a complex individual who impressed different people in different ways. One woman claimed, "He was a very cranky little man.... I don't think I have ever seen him smile." A friend, however, noted that he "had a very good sense of humour. He could see things that nobody else could see." When officials from the Carnegie Corporation came to Canso, he arranged for them to see Carrie, his maid, in the rectory room reading the *New Russian Primer*, a high school textbook from the Soviet Union praising the wonders of the Five-Year Plan. "He was a dramatic rogue," said a visitor. "He'd do stuff like that."

Even the way he sat attracted attention. "He didn't sit like other people," a woman recalled. "He wound his legs around a chair or his cane. It was as if he was coiling up, seeking to control his restless energy."

Father Jimmy seldom relaxed, never played cards, gave up smoking, had no time for small talk.

One day he sent word to a priest to come to a fishermen's meeting. When the man wired back: "Have a funeral on my hands tomorrow," Father Jimmy replied: "Let the dead bury the dead. Come to the meeting."

Father Jimmy's provocative questions pointed the way to a better life for the poor fishermen. His friend Leo MacIntyre described his work in Canso:

"When people approached him with a problem he drew them into discussion on it in an effort to get them to diagnose it for themselves. When a certain solution was suggested he helped and encouraged....

"He wanted people to get, as it were, a vision of the way they could function in society if they could learn to work with their fellows. Once a person had glimpsed this outlook he felt he would no longer return to his old way of life. He was fully aware that most of the problems which his people had to cope with were economic; yet economic activity was not the final end of Adult Education.

"The fishermen in Father Jimmy's small parish

at Canso were in a bad way when he arrived there. Poorly paid, they were often lacking even in the ambition to help themselves. It took time, faith and much perseverance on his part to arouse even a flicker of interest in these people."

Leo Ward, an American priest who visited Nova Scotia in 1939 and wrote a book on it, described the province as "The Land of Cooperation."

"It is the hardest thing in the world to have faith in man, and to keep it up. So says Father Jimmy Tompkins, the famous Nova Scotia cooperator...." In a chapter entitled "The Little Common Fellow," he described him:

"Every day Father Tompkins is going, every day and half the night. Such an insistent man, tiring all others out, but himself never tiring. He is talking, he is pushing and urging, he is hoping and waiting, he is at times even complaining and saying that people are no good—a thing he does not and cannot believe...."

Ward called the priest "a pesky little man...an ornery little fellow, a cantankerous sort of man." But, he added,

"[Father Jimmy]...has the main tool and asset, the one without which he could not do a thing. This is faith in the people and love of them, an uncalculating faith and love. They love and trust him without end, because he first loves and trusts them without end. Between him and them, we see the model instance of cooperation, and the principle of all cooperation."

FATHER JIMMY URGED his parishioners and anyone else interested in bringing about change to think for themselves. He organized study clubs and regular Saturday meetings where a dedicated few began to make sense of their world and their woes.

And he wouldn't let other people relax. One visitor told of waking up at six in the morning, and finding Father Jimmy sitting at the side of his bed, reading *The New York Times*, doubtless seeking some piece of information to stimulate his guest.

Of himself, Tompkins said: "I don't think anybody around here can say with certainty whether I am a Liberal or a Tory. Personally, I'd rather be a Mosaic Radical—for God and the people—not saying that a good Tory or a good Grit, for that matter, might not also be for both."

Life in the small fishing communities, and the miseries of many who lived there on the bare edge of existence, largely escaped the public eye in the 1920s. Then in 1927, Canso suddenly became the focus of provincial and national attention. While other Canadians cheered the 60th anniversary of Confederation in cities and towns, men on the Canso docks wondered publicly what *they* had to celebrate. And with the help of their parish priest, Father Jimmy Tompkins, their cries and concerns reached the ears of powerful people in Canada.

CHAPTER FOUR

The Vital Presence

"Organization is the fruit of intelligence, of knowledge, and without education we feel sure that cooperation would be built on sand."

Father Jimmy Tompkins

A MYTHOLOGY HAS GROWN UP about that day in Canso. It claims that Father Jimmy organized a meeting on the dock, the fishermen protested their plight, and the federal government quickly set up a royal commission to investigate and ameliorate it. In fact, it took a great deal of pressure from many sources to persuade Ottawa to act.

A fisherman grumbled to Father Jimmy that July 1st "wasn't much of a jubilee"—what did he and his fellows have to celebrate?

The men who milled around on the dock at Canso on that 60th anniversary of the creation of Canada could have simply dispersed, grumbling, going back home, taking up their usual tasks on the following day, finding nothing changed.

But Father Jimmy proved to be the vital presence, and his five and a half years of urging, nagging, needling, animating bore fruit on that day. The events of July 1, 1927, served as the trigger for what became known as the Antigonish Movement. One man, a few gifted leaders, a mass of discontented fishermen at the bottom of the social heap came together in a remote part of Canada and acted in a way that benefited them—and others.

"What have we to celebrate?"

In his characteristic way, the priest asked the man why fishermen didn't call a meeting to air their complaints. "It's a holiday," Father Jimmy said, "and everybody's ashore." The man followed up on the suggestion.

At seven that evening, Father Jimmy phoned John Chafe: "There's a meeting on in the hall. I'm afraid of trouble. Will you come?"

When he arrived, the assembled multitude asked Chafe to chair it. The proceedings wavered between protest and patriotism. One man jumped up and shouted: "What have *we* to cheer about?" The year had been a good one for the fisheries—but not for the fishermen. Good weather had persisted in the Atlantic, and large hauls of fish landed, depressing prices.

As the meeting progressed, the fishermen wondered whether it was treason to talk as they did about their problems on a day of national rejoicing. Father Jimmy stayed on the sidelines, taking no part in the discussions. Fishermen stood up, and each told the same story. They could not feed their children. Blame for this lay with the big trawlers that were ruining their meagre livelihoods.

After listening to their grievances, Chafe suggested that the meeting petition the federal government to send representatives to Canso. Surely if they saw the deplorable way people lived here, they would do something to alleviate it. A document was drawn up, replete with "whereases" and "therefores," and taken to Father Jimmy for his approval. He snorted, "You're not lawyers. You're fishermen. So write like fishermen. Just ask them when the hell they are going to do something for us."

According to Chafe, the priest "wrote in a few 'hells' and 'damns' of his own."

At the parish house, Chafe met two former students of Father Jimmy who did some newspaper reporting on the side. One sent a story to the *Halifax Herald* about the Canso meeting. It ran under the headline, "Revolution in Canso," and the paper sent a reporter to the town to find out more about what had happened on July 1st. His story did not appear in the paper. And the federal government simply ignored the petition from the meeting.

It looked as if the protest had been in vain.

Father Jimmy decided to act.

He wired the *Herald* offering to buy a full page of advertising in the paper to tell the story of Canso. In 1927, the Liberals were in power in Ottawa and the federal government controlled the fisheries. Although the *Herald* supported the Conservatives who formed the government in Nova Scotia, its editors stalled: a story on the plight of fishermen might do Canso more harm than good.

So Father Jimmy phoned the *Halifax Chronicle*, urging the paper to send someone down to Canso. An editor arrived, and returned to Halifax to break the story of the discontent in the community a few days later. It roused the government from its torpor. A delegation from the Fisheries Department in Ottawa, accompanied by William Duff, the local M.P., held a meeting in Canso. Duff launched into his speech. An unknown voice shouted, "Now Duff, no bluff!"

Then Dr. Pound, the Deputy Minister of the Fisheries Department, tried to blind his listeners with science. He defended the operations of trawlers, and spoke in great detail about marine life, stunning and intimidating the audience. To this bureaucrat, the problems in the fisheries were simply technical, not human—with a few adjustments at the edges, all would be well.

No fisherman stood up to question or confront the visiting expert. Then a woman reporter from the *Herald*, which had decided that the Canso story *was* news, spoke up. Pound's speech had been most interesting, she said. But what did marine flora and fauna have to do with undernourishment on the Canso Coast? The fishermen, taking courage from her stand, poured out their grievances.

The meeting ended, the visitors departed.

Ottawa had responded to the request of the fishermen.

A meeting had been held in Canso.

But Father Jimmy was not satisfied; something more than political posturing and scientific and bureaucratic mystification was needed if life in the community was to improve.

SHORTLY AFTER THE MEETING, the diocesan priests held their annual retreat in Antigonish. The perpetual problem of rural decline cropped up in their discussions. Then Father Jimmy spoke. It was good to do something for the farmers. But what about the fishermen? One priest claimed that the price of fish was high enough to give them a good living. Father Jimmy told the assembly what the fishermen received for their catches on the wharf. Then he called together priests from other coastal communities. Forty of them signed a petition to Ottawa demanding the immediate appointment of a royal commission to investigate the inshore fisheries.

The priests of 1927, literate, knowledgeable about the problems of their people, aware of the power of the press, represented one of the few forces in the diocese that could articulate the views of the poor. Returning to their parishes, the priests wrote to newspapers and sent telegrams to Halifax and Ottawa, urging the politicians to act. Father Alex Boudreau from Petit-de-Grat wrote to the *Chronicle*, demanding that something be done.

The federal and provincial governments, under pressure from the large, integrated fishing companies and the Halifax merchants who had ready access to the corridors of power, favoured the status quo. The protesting fishermen, a bunch of rowdies, stood in the way of progress in the industry. Yet they had secured the support of clergy and the press, and so perhaps their problems were worthy of study and immediate action.

On October 7, 1927, the Governor General of Canada, by order in council, authorized the establishment of the Royal Commission on the Fisheries of the Maritime Provinces and the Magdalen Islands. The Hon. A.K. MacLean, president of the Exchequer Court, chaired the five-member body, which included three men from the region and a university professor from Montreal. The MacLean Commission held forty-nine meetings in the region, and heard 823 witnesses. It made public what the people in the Maritimes already knew, and the media spread the stories of the plight of the fishermen across Canada.

After the meeting in Canso, the big fish companies tried to calm the storm by claiming that the free market would solve the problems of the low prices offered for catches. H.F. Robinson, in a telegram, assured the Canso fishermen when they pleaded for better prices: "Matter having our careful consideration, and price will be increased at earliest date market will stand it."

The MacLean Commission soon lost any faith that its members might have had in the hidden hands of private enterprise assuaging the ills that witnesses poured out before them. They heard that steam trawlers, scooping up the bounty of the sea, also hauled in immature fish, and the spawn of cod and haddock—predictions that soon the fishing grounds would be barren. Fishermen claimed that fish caught with hooks were better, their flesh firmer than those caught by "sea scavengers" which hauled in crushed and flabby catches. Inshore fishermen received as little as sixty cents for a hundred pounds of cod.

John Kennedy, president of the Fishermen's Federation of Nova Scotia, addressed the commission on October 29, 1927. For the past four years, his crew of four had each earned only $600 a year. "Now it is impossible for us people to maintain our families...." Kennedy attacked the trawlers. Manned by foreigners, they glutted the market—and paid no taxes. Others complained that these large vessels destroyed the nets of inshore fishermen.

An investigative reporter from the *Chronicle* fleshed out the work of the commission with a series entitled "Save Our Fishermen." He told of workers at the Maritime Fish Corporation earning two dollars a day for a ten-hour stint. Out of their twelve dollars a week, they paid seven dollars every seven weeks for rubber boots. Employment in the plant was never certain: the workers had to come to the gate, gloves in hand, every morning, even if they were not needed on that day. Anyone complaining about the miserable conditions under which they worked would be fired—and have no hope of finding another job in the community.

The biggest companies could afford technologies that took the largest harvests from the sea and maximized their profits. The inshore fishermen followed a way of life that had changed little over the centuries. Even if they had the capital to improve their operations, they lacked the skills and expertise to use new techniques and make more money from what they caught.

Some small efforts had been made to reach and encourage the inshore fishermen. In the mid-1920s, the Biological Board in Halifax had sought to interest fishermen in improved methods, the commission pointed out, focusing on the conservation of lobsters and technical matters. In 1926, the Atlantic Experimental Station sent an instructor along the Eastern Shore of Nova Scotia to teach fishermen about processing dried fish. The Antigonish diocese raised funds for scholarships for fishermen. But these small efforts did little to change things fundamentally.

The MacLean Commission reported on May 4, 1928, in a 115-page document that painted a grim picture of empty harbours, idle boats and discouraged fishermen:

"[The fisherman's] toil has too often carried a maximum of hardship and a minimum of reward. His work has been carried on under conditions incredibly bad. Primitive methods of marketing have been followed. There has been little or no cooperation. In many parts, transportation has been difficult. There have been few technical educational facilities, such as are available to other industries. The shore fishery has drifted along in a happy-go-lucky, go-as-you-please manner and the individual shore fisherman has worked in his own way, often to his own disadvantage. For this condition he must, in fairness, accept some share of the responsibility. There has been no organization through which he could deal with large and complex problems and interests. He has not learned, like wage earners in other industries, to protect himself by organization and cooperation. He still sells, haphazardly, at a low level of prices and buys at a high level of retail cost. He has had therefore no power whatsoever of bargaining; and having little to say about the selling of his product, unlike other producers he has been forced to take whatever price he could get—a price sometimes below the actual cost of production."

The commission hammered home a theme dear to the heart of Father Jimmy and his followers:

"From the history of organized labour in the cities, and in other industries, the fishers should perhaps have learned long ago the value of cooperation. They must now lose the old idea that they are isolated producers running separate industries and competing with one another; they must replace it with the thought that each is a unit in one great corporation."

Towards the end of the report, the commission painted a grim picture of conditions among the people from whom they had heard and of the places in which they lived:

"We were given vivid word-pictures and visited fishing villages in which aging men alone were left to man the fishing boats, with little hope of adequate livelihood in the future years of their physical incapacity, and no hope of pension such as is possible to workers in other industries; of fishing communities from which the young men had emigrated in large numbers to another land; or were hoping to emigrate when they could gather sufficient means; of neglected boats with hulls ripe and rotten on the beach; of discarded gear once valuable and useful, but now falling to decay, of abandoned fishing vessels, left hopefully equipped as they came in from the sea, to wait a better season that never came; of wharves and breakwaters once staunch and busy, but now dilapidated and deserted; of once prosperous localities slowly but surely becoming the graveyards of a dead industry; of fisherfolk despondent and disheartened, struggling on against economic disabilities, eager to labour in one of the most hazardous of pursuits but unable to sell their products for a reasonable reward, always hoping for better luck, and clinging grimly and patiently to their calling—a tribute at once to their character and their courage; and of schoolchildren psychologically distrustful of a future in their own country and planning to migrate at maturity to another land to make a living."

The commission favoured direct government

involvement in upgrading the skills of inshore fishermen, believing that a "practical system of education would be regarded with sympathy by fishermen, and that some form of education should be devised under the Department, in cooperation with Provincial Departments of Education...." It noted that, "What had been done for agricultural education is an interesting example of what might be done for fishery education."

The commission suggested that "universities of the Maritime Provinces might consider the possibilities of aiding any effort in behalf of the fishermen's education." Extension courses could do this.

The commission recommended cold storage facilities in fishing communities, improved transportation, and the provision of bait freezers. And all its members agreed on the need for upgrading and inspecting fish to improve its quality, and a system of loans to fishermen for boats and gear.

But the commission split over the issue of steam trawlers, with four members demanding that they be banned from Canadian ports and forbidden to land fish at them. MacLean's minority report defended the trawlers. The government set a limit on the number of trawlers, but in reality the trawler fleet continued to grow.

At its meeting in Halifax, the commission had asked Father Moses Coady to testify. His brief suggested a threefold approach to resolving the crisis in the fisheries: organization of inshore fishermen and their involvement in formulating industry policy; the use of science and technology in the fisheries; and the promotion of producer and consumer cooperatives.

The commission accepted the last suggestion, urging that "the establishment of cooperative organizations of fishermen be assisted by the Department as soon as possible, and that an organizer, experienced in cooperative methods, be appointed and paid by the Federal Government for the required period to initiate and complete this work."

THE MACLEAN COMMISSION report appeared at a critical time. At the Sixth Rural Conference on October 8-9, 1928, Tompkins, Coady and others reviewed the recommendations of the Royal Commission in the presence of one of its members, J.G. Robichaud. Fathers Michael Gillis and Leo J. Keats made a recommendation that would prove historic:

"That whereas the economic well-being of a people to a large extent depends on their acquaintance with economic history and economic and sociological forces at work in a country; And whereas it is believed that the common worker is exploited now, because of lack of knowledge of these forces and principles; And whereas the time would now appear opportune for the adoption of adult education for the whole of Canada and particularly for the Maritime Provinces; Therefore, be it resolved that we pledge our support to the organization that would in the opinion of a committee to be appointed by the conference, best formulate the policy of

Adult Education; And be it further resolved that this conference authorize the proper agencies in this problem."

In the following month, the Board of Governors of St. F.X. adopted unanimously a resolution approving "the establishment of Extension work in connection with the University...." It also asked that "arrangements be made as soon as possible to provide a man for the carrying out of this work." Moses Coady was the man. He had been training for the job all his life. As far back as 1915, Tompkins had written to his cousin, telling him that he would become an "inspiring" leader, and encouraging him to learn "elocution" and "good talking."

Coady had done a lot of "good talking" and organizing since receiving that letter. He had trained in Rome, taught at St. F.X., organized the Nova Scotia Teachers' Union and studied adult education in the United States and Western Canada, concluding that the "Maritimes will have to work out its own salvation."

From 1929, the figure of Father Moses Coady dominated the Antigonish Movement. In bringing about social change, he had a markedly different style from Father Jimmy. Very different physically, Coady resembled a great pillar of probity and reliability, an anchor in troubled times. His strong, impressive voice tended to calm people, whereas Father Jimmy's voice was squeaky and he always looked pale, small and fragile.

Father Jimmy talked to individuals, badgered

and upset them, prodded them toward action—"a barb," wrote George Boyle, "a spur." Coady preferred speeches to the masses; he was a charismatic leader who used his masterly oratory and spoke with absolute certainty: "If you feed this kind of hen with this kind of feed, she can't help but lay a lot of eggs."

Father Jimmy entrusted people with ideas. He read ceaselessly, handed out books and publications, let ordinary people give these ideas hands and feet. Brilliant, irascible, anarchist in spirit—Tompkins was utterly incapable of orchestrating a system for social and economic reform. Although Father Coady was not an original and unconventional thinker, he laid down guidelines for others to follow. His speeches and letters are full of blueprints and formulae for democracy. Tompkins, on the other hand, rejected blueprints, forever urging those who listened to him to read what others had written and make up their own minds about what ailed the land.

Coady would say, "I'll organize you." Tompkins would say, "Organize yourself."

Tompkins' ideas and actions inspired the Antigonish Movement. But he always kept his distance from it, and often criticized its approach and activities.

One critic of Tompkins claimed that "he was in a way like a mathematician trying to solve problems and it seems to me *that* was the problem. He didn't see that synthesizing these peripheral things would result in a solution. He was narrow in that sense."

The strength of Coady's approach lay in his ability to inspire and focus people.

THE MACLEAN COMMISSION was only the last of several initiatives that resulted in an effective Extension Department at St. F.X. and the emergence from Extension of what would be called the Antigonish Movement.

An earlier important effort was that of the Scottish Catholic Society of Canada. That society developed out of the flurry of interest in preserving the Gaelic language, provoked by Father Tompkins' achievements for the Acadians. The Antigonish Highland Society had already asked St. F.X. to establish a chair in Gaelic, but was told that that was impractical. Then the Scottish Catholic Society, formed in 1919 out of a group that petitioned the Nova Scotia government for Gaelic in the public schools, pressured the university to provide extension services, even offering financial support. Father Coady felt the society's move "scared" the bishop and St. F.X. into action. Coady also pointed to Father Michael Gillis' work through the Scottish Catholic Society and on his own, as "perhaps the most responsible for the Extension Department at St. F.X." Gillis was "the creative mind behind all movements, the dynamic leader and inspirer" who pressured older leaders, including Hugh MacPherson and Jimmy Tompkins himself.

Yet another force was the St. F.X. Alumni Association brief of 1928, calling for a chair in Rural Education and Rural Sociology and a basic program for social action in eastern Nova Scotia aimed at farmers, fishermen and miners. The brief pointed out that this would reinforce wide support for the university among average citizens, it would carry forward spiritual principles and address social and economic problems exposed by the royal commissions on coal (1926) and the fisheries (1927).

It was at that point that the new Department of Fisheries (recommended by the MacLean Commission) asked Coady to take on the massive assignment of organizing the fishermen of eastern Canada. Coady held his first meeting in Canso, addressing 600 fishermen and their wives in the Ideal Theatre. Then he set off to travel 13,000 kilometres in ten months, holding up to four meetings a day with fishermen. In June, 1930, 208 delegates from fishing villages in the region came to a meeting in Halifax at the request of Father Coady. Here they founded the United Maritime Fishermen as a collective marketing agency.

THE REPORT of the Royal Commission, with its emphasis on organization, cooperation and extension education, vindicated Father Jimmy's views regarding cooperatives. According to Mary Laben, a woman who knew him well, the little priest "had one direction in life and that was to push everyone towards co-ops."

On September 18, 1929, he wrote to George

Keen, secretary, the Cooperative Union of Canada:

"Today the humblest kind of work must fail unless it has knowledge and ideas in it—and here I include organization. Without these work is only slavery.... Let the modern workman but learn about industry, adding the mind to the body in it, and then his brute strength, hitherto without mind in its slavery, has new eyes put into it, and even something of a soul.... Then his work itself becomes an education and a delight, with a moral centre of gravity in itself, and our man goes forward in his normal strength abreast with the world that has so far trampled over his unnecessary and abnormal weakness."

After organizing the U.M.F., Father Coady and his colleagues began to set up study groups as the first step in creating credit unions and cooperatives. The great achievement of what became known as the Antigonish Movement—which might just as easily have been dubbed the Canso Movement, since it started there—was the way in which adult education was linked to the formation of local organizations that gave people control over their lives through cooperation. The nickels and dimes collected for the credit unions provided capital for cooperatives, generating a sense in small communities that they could tackle their own problems with their own resources. Father Coady commented:

"I built the cooperatives not to give jobs to our people but to give the people who stayed on the land a chance to get their fair share of the national income. The principal thing was not the cooperative. The principal thing was the life that came out of it for those who belonged to the working classes and for the primary producing classes, such as farmers, fishermen and lumbermen."

But Father Tompkins wrote: "Cooperation. I don't like the word. The merchants think it's trying to put them out of business, and people often think it's just handing peas and beans and bologna over the counter. It's a spirit: that's the most important thing about it."

Cooperatives were not new in Nova Scotia; the first had been established in Stellarton in 1861. But organizing fisheries cooperatives presented very different challenges from setting up consumer-based ventures in towns. The Webbs, the gurus of the British cooperative movement, had asserted that workers could not organize cooperatives to sell what they produced. How could poverty-stricken, isolated fisherfolk possibly compete with large, powerful companies in the so-called free market?

The Antigonish Movement had strong ethical impulses and did more than set up study groups and hand out pamphlets on how to start co-ops and credit unions. Local tensions had to be managed, people had to be convinced of the necessity to work together. Poor workers had to understand the reasons for their plight—and take responsibility for making a better life for themselves, their families, their communities. Age-old patterns of dependency had to be broken.

FATHER JIMMY DIDN'T WAIT for St. F.X.'s Extension Division to start a cooperative in Dover, a huddle of hovels along a barely passable street. In 1928, Bishop Morrison sent Father Poirier from D'Escousse to Canso to serve as Father Jimmy's curate. This calm young man became like a son to the priest, and they spent six years together, time Poirier saw as a postgraduate course in unique ways of learning. As the curate took over some of the routine priestly duties, Father Jimmy moved into action. His activities among the fishermen of the Canso coast had drawn unwelcome attention to Dover. A government official took one look at the place and recommended that its residents be evacuated. Nothing could have challenged Father Jimmy more!

For two years, under his tutelage, fishermen studied and saved their dimes. Then forty of them founded the Dover Lobster Cooperative with $128 in capital, and began marketing the lobsters they caught themselves, rather than relying on middlemen. No one would give the group credit.

In a letter to Dr. F.P. Keppel of the Carnegie Corporation, Father Jimmy commented wryly, "I'm supposed to be thinking spiritually instead of talking lobsters."

He called on his friend John Chafe, who told the co-op members that they had assets—"Timber, axes, time, and now you're working together as a group." Father Jimmy suggested they build their own cannery.

In those days, small lobsters went into cans, large ones directly to market. The priest lent the group $300, and arranged a loan of another $700 from a private individual at a low rate of interest. The fishermen went into the woods, cut down trees, hauled the logs out by hand, and found stones for the foundation of their building. Equipment from idle lobster plants, bought at low cost, was installed, and the venture began with "more faith than facilities," as John Chafe put it. Within two months, the co-op members were able to pay themselves half a cent a pound above the going rate for lobsters, and owned a plant worth $5,280, debt free.

On July 7, 1932, Father Jimmy wrote to Dr. Keppel:

"I was instrumental in starting a factory in a little village called Dover among poor people last fall.... The venture was a real success and we put up 435 cases, just the lobsters caught by themselves. You could almost jump from the factory to the furthest lobster pot so you see the quality was excellent. We sold them for seventeen dollars a case. The last 235 cases we sold for sixteen dollars a case F.O.B. Halifax. That, of course, is entirely too little. Still, we made a go of it and put the proposition on its feet. These poor fellows did not have a cent last fall.... They put about two thousand dollars worth of free labour into the proposition. They are now preparing to go to the woods to get the material for a little factory in which to put up boneless cod."

Five days later, he again wrote to Dr. Keppel, telling him that he'd sent him half a dozen cans of "our Dover lobsters." Then he told how cooperation had transformed this village of forty families:

"They paid every dollar of the expenses, paid the current price for the lobsters, gave a bonus of one half cent a pound or a ten per cent bonus to the casual workers. They have to the good somewhere around one hundred dollars. We reckon that they are better off...to the extent of about four thousand dollars than they would have been had they sold their lobsters in the old way. I went to visit them last Saturday with a friend who acted as a sort of finance minister. We distributed more money than was ever seen at one time in Dover. We had among the money about twenty fifty-dollar bills. I doubt if a fifty-dollar bill was ever seen in Dover before."

Father Jimmy does not mention his hard work, the Saturday meetings that attracted only fifteen people at first, the search for funds, the fight against illiteracy, the combined efforts that created the first good street in the village.

Fired by success, the people of Dover built two new fishing smacks and, in 1933, their own fish-curing plant and storage plant. Through their own stores, they saved four dollars on each fishing net, five cents a pound on nails, fifteen cents on a bushel of potatoes. Families grew vegetables on unused plots of ground. By 1934, the entire village was enrolled in study clubs, and everyone had become a reader.

On January 12, 1934, Father Tompkins wrote to Kay Thompson, one of Coady's secretaries and a key person in the Antigonish Movement, telling her that "study clubs are breaking loose all over the landscape down here. Things are moving fast." All this, as the little priest noted in his inimitable way, would "rupture the blood vessel" of "some exploiters around here."

In the depths of the Great Depression, the Blue Ribbon Canners of Dover, operated by the co-op society, had a turnover of $10,000 a year. Father Jimmy travelled to Boston to find buyers for its output.

Tompkins also went to Edmonton to visit Ned Corbett, a fellow Nova Scotian. Corbett headed the Extension Department of the University of Alberta, which, like that of St. F.X., received funding from the Carnegie Corporation. It used theatre as a way of generating community development, and had the most modern technology to reach learners in isolated areas. Corbett recalled how enthusiastic his visitor had been about the University of Alberta's extension program, but added that "he put his finger upon the weakness of our whole programme....

"We were dealing with an almost wholly receptive people. We were not succeeding in getting people to think and study and plan together to solve their own problems."

Father Jimmy advised Corbett:

"For your program you've got to get hold of the little fellow. The little fellow, together, is a giant; they make giants. You've got to give them ideas...."

FATHER COADY BELIEVED that "Dr. Tompkins' idealism did not prevent him from having a practical business sense. He kept the financial affairs of his parish in excellent condition; and even in the realm of ideas, although he examined many, Dr. Tompkins would choose the most workable one in the end. He was progressive and radical, even to the point of revolution, yet as realistic and conservative as a director of the Bank of England."

One of Tompkins' skills lay in his ability to identify the "little fellows"—men like William "Billy Tom" Feltmate, Brian Meagher, and Alfred Hanlon, who all lived in and near Canso; and later, in Reserve Mines, raw material like Joe Laben and Jimmy Marsh—and to encourage them to make the best use of their abilities. He would support them, but he would also expect these able people to find solutions for themselves and their communities.

He recognized the valuable role that women could play in dealing with health problems in Canso. One of his affluent parishioners, A. Sampson, gave him two large double dwellings, and Tompkins wrote to Mother Faustina, former General Superior of the Sisters of Saint Martha, asking for her help to get some nuns sent to Canso:

"I must be honest with you, I cannot offer anything but fish, fog and fornication."

Mother Faustina was then in Western Canada. When she returned to Antigonish, she carried the request to General Superior Mother Ignatius, and Mother Faustina and Sisters Denis Marie and Mary

Concepta arrived in Canso in 1933, their presence not entirely welcomed by Protestant residents. Apparently Father Jimmy left them to find their own way in the community. They began visiting families to find out what they needed, making lists of what these people lacked. Soon the Mother House in Antigonish was sending food, not only for the nuns, but extra for distribution in the community. They also sent scrap material. The sisters began to teach the women knitting, sewing, dying, methods of making over older clothes—whatever local women wanted to learn.

The courage of the Sisters of Saint Martha was at least equal to that of Tompkins. While this order was established to provide domestic service, especially for St. Francis Xavier University, they had done some social work, in hospitals and in the homes of sick people. With Father Jimmy in Canso the demand was for creative social action, and the sisters took on this work in the face of desperate poverty and bigotry. They had to convince the Protestants that they were there to help and not to indoctrinate.

The sisters read to Father Jimmy during meals to save him time, with the priest commenting at length on what he heard. A small grant from the Carnegie Corporation enabled him, with the help of Sister Denis Marie, the youngest, to open a library in one of the donated buildings. It included works of fiction as well as practical publications. Years later, Sister Denis Marie said that she was literally wallowing in stacks of magazines and books and pamphlets, cataloguing the library, while an exuberant Father Jimmy threw open its doors and ran around the community shouting, "The library is open! The library is open!"

Tompkins irritated the nuns. He couldn't stay on one subject, was forever finding more things for them to do—but he treated them like fellow crusaders, gave them new, invigorating work, won admiration, and established lasting friendships with many of them. He had given them an opportunity to live and work in difficult circumstances, overcome intolerance, and fight poverty. They had the courage to do the work, and loved Father Tompkins for giving them such a defining chance.

TOMPKINS KEPT UP HIS CRITICISMS of big, absentee business. Kingsley Brown, a newspaper reporter, recalled a misty street-corner conversation with Father Jimmy in 1932: "Every time you buy a pound of beef there is a nickel going to J. Pierpont Morgan. You can't get a nickel cigar but a few cents go to J. Pierpont Morgan."

As word of his work spread, the priest began to receive visits from radicals and reformers. E.J. Garland, an Alberta M.P. and agrarian radical, came to the community and impressed Tompkins. They began to correspond. Garland sent his friend copies of his speeches on unemployment in the House of Commons. Father Jimmy delighted in what he learned from Garland, and quoted from him to jolt people. On October 18, 1928, Garland wrote to the priest:

"I have heard farmers repeat again and again with caustic bitterness—'What's the use of teaching us to farm when we are being driven off the farms by economic oppression?' The first things necessary then appeared to be to improve the financial position of our people and that has only been possible through organization and cooperation."

Garland and Tompkins, kindred spirits from very different social and geographical backgrounds, recognized the need for people at the local level to act together rather than expecting salvation to come from government.

Under the guidance of the little priest the people of the Canso coast in Guysborough County more and more came alive to their potential as they came together to discuss the roots of their problems and what they themselves could do about them.

IN SEARCHING FOR WAYS to strengthen local economies, Father Jimmy became interested in the idea of "people's banks." In 1864, the farmers in Rustico, on Prince Edward Island, had set up their own bank with the help of another remarkable priest, the Abbé Belcourt. It lost its charter in 1883, after the federal government began to close down small banks. But this initiative inspired Alphonse Desjardins, who organized the first *caisse populaire* in Lévis, Québec, in 1900. Father Jimmy became interested in this movement around 1924;

priests played a key role in the operations of the *caisses populaires.*

At a rural conference in Antigonish, he suggested that Roy Bergengren be invited to the next one. Many people from Quebec had migrated to New England to work in the factories there, taking with them the concept of locally owned and controlled people's banks. The exodus of Nova Scotians to the Boston States had forged strong linkages between the two areas. E. A. Filene, a Boston businessman, supported the credit union movement in the 1920s. Roy Bergengren worked with him. In the United States, the Credit Union National Extension Bureau assisted in the creation of people's banks by securing supportive legislation in individual states.

Fathers Tompkins and Coady asked Bergengren to prepare similar legislation to be presented to the Nova Scotia government. Ontario and Quebec already had enabling legislation, but only in Quebec was it widely used. A Credit Union Act became law in Nova Scotia in April, 1932—the third one in Canada. A very progressive act for Canada in the 1930s, the legislation in Nova Scotia permitted any seven citizens living in a specific neighbourhood or belonging to an occupation or an institution to form a credit union.

Father Coady recalled how, "but for a snowstorm, Canso would have had the first credit union in Nova Scotia. In the Canso era Dr. Tompkins laid the foundation for the credit union and the library movement. He is the father of both as far as the Maritime Provinces of Canada are concerned."

"But for a snowstorm...." In the fall of 1932, Roy Bergengren and A.B. MacDonald, the assistant director of St. Francis Xavier's Extension Department, set out for Canso. A snowstorm diverted them to Cape Breton, and there they met with Father Coady and a group of miners in Reserve Mines who decided to form a credit union, the first in the province. Three more sprang up on the island: in Broad Cove, Inverness and Sydney. The first two were community-based; the one in Sydney was started by gas, electric and streetcar workers.

By the end of 1935, Nova Scotia had forty-five credit unions. The one in Antigonish is named after Roy Bergengren.

As usual, Father Jimmy put the case for credit unions plainly: "You simply take what extra money you have—the savings in your sock—and let your neighbours use it for a while, only you don't demand his right arm for security."

More and more, during the 1930s, ordinary people took heart and began to organize. In Whitehead, twenty kilometres from Canso, people "were pressed so hard against the wall...that it was impossible to get any closer. So we had to turn and face the enemy." They organized to buy supplies in bulk at better rates. Then four of them took a risk, shipping a crate of lobsters to a buyer in Boston whose name they picked from a fishing gazette. At the wharf, these fishermen usually received $9.80

for a crate of lobsters. They thought the Boston buyer had made a mistake when they got back a cheque for $32.00.

Father Jimmy spoke to the American Catholic Rural Conference in October, 1935:

"Take credit unions. They make for the federation of man, and are great aids to Christianity. They, with cooperative stores, prevent the work of loan sharks, eye-gougers, graft, undue profits, exploitation, and give us honesty in quality and quantity of goods. These two movements alone would help greatly in building a world *naturaliter Christiana*. At present we are rowing against the current."

Through the early 1930s, he continued to travel around his parish, pockets bulging with leaflets, pamphlets, clippings and all manner of publication, urging people to think, talk, meet, organize. He became a frequent presence at United Maritime Fishermen rallies and gatherings along the Guysborough Coast, teaming up with his fellow activists, Father Keats from St. Peter's in Cape Breton and Father Charles Forest of Larry's River near Antigonish. Father Jimmy gave the people of Dover not only heart—but resources. They showed that even the poorest of the poor could make better lives for themselves through collective effort.

In a document titled, "Economic Co-operation and the Churches," Father Jimmy sent out a clarion call to all the clergy:

"It is not only wise but inevitably a matter of

duty for the churches to foster co-operation. Christians cannot escape the obligation of forsaking the dog-eat-dog system under which we are living. There is no foundation in Christian morals or ethics for a system which entitles one man to live off and exploit his neighbours. A man is entitled to remuneration for services rendered his fellow men and nothing more. That is the very cornerstone of co-operation.

"To fight the enemies of humanity in the modern world it is necessary to have modern weapons. Now natural human relations suggest that one of the most suitable and efficient weapons would be co-operation. Religious minded people cannot escape the conclusion that they should accept this weapon, no matter how much it may cut across their own selfish interest or those of their friends. They should follow their principles to the logical conclusion."

Tompkins had seen an article by a staff correspondent of the *Halifax Herald*, Kingsley Brown. He shot off a letter:

"You could get great 'copy' down in these parts.... Here is a story that came to me a few minutes ago: A man from Little Dover [six miles from Canso] walked to Canso today. On his way he met a man *from* Canso with an axe on his shoulder. The Dover fellow said, 'You are going to cut wood?' 'No,' said the man, 'I am going to Dover to give you fellows a few days on your new fish store.' Dover is now on a *new* cooperative venture, a fish store—it is one of a number. They are all sold 100% on working together."

Father Jimmy knew a good story, constantly watched for an exciting reporter—and he knew the clinchers: "It happens that Dover is almost entirely Catholic. The man from Canso is Ralph Fanning, a Baptist, and one of our most respected citizens."

And Father Jimmy went on in the letter, already trying to frame Brown's article: "Give people a chance, tell them the truth and give them a square deal and they will all work together. Laissez-Faire, Everybody for himself etc has broken up the solidarity of the human race.... While that lasts the world has to prepare for Communism.... Come to Canso. When you do please come and stay with me."

And the bright young reporter, who had been praised for not feeding his readers "baloney," was on his way. Kingsley Brown teamed up with barnstormer Humph Wadden and flew to Dover in Wadden's Gypsy Moth airplane, equipped with skis for landing on ice. Out of that visit came extraordinary promotion of the achievements in Father Tompkin's parish—clippings to send to other reformers and potential financial supporters; clippings to help keep the fire alive at home.

How could the world not respond to the enthusiasm of Kingsley Brown's 1934 articles? Brown wrote in the *Halifax Herald*:

"Little Dover doesn't wait for prosperity on corners.... Little Dover is setting the pace, culturally, industrially, and socially. Little Dover is not only on the road to recovery, she is half way there....

"Grasping a brand new idea, convinced that nothing could be worse than what they were suffering, they struck out for salvation—and are finding it.

"The Little Dover Co-operative Lobster Cannery...is group-owned by the people of Little Dover, started two years ago and catering chiefly to the British market. Here is part of the annual report (for 1933): 'Encouraged by the success of our plant we have taken steps to extend our activities into other branches of the fishing industry. A building is now being erected to take care of curing various kinds of fish and studies are being made in methods of processing and market requirements.... The beneficial influence of our company on the lives of the people of this locality is now so obvious that it is the duty of every resident to enlarge their interests by studying and applying the principles of co-operation on which the company is founded and conducted.'

"$1000 had been paid in bonuses to shareholders as well as to casual laborers; a dividend of 6 per cent was declared—apart from the bonus—and $1,400 was re-invested in the company. That is the way group action has worked in Little Dover, where, in the past, one private enterprise after another has folded up a failure....

"Virtually everything in Little Dover is sold 'at cost.' The word 'profit' has almost vanished from the vocabulary of the Little Doverite....

"The day of illiteracy is gone.... Night and day the little high school is busy.... In their homes they read the *New York Times* or the *New York Herald-Tribune*....

"Prof. John Tait on the faculty of McGill University...spends a considerable period each year studying the remarkable revolution which is taking place in these counties....

"Last week some of the young men of Little Dover sent to the high school students of Canso a challenge to a debate.... Be 'Resolved that Nova Scotia's economic ills are the fault not of geographical position nor of its economic status in Confederation, but the fault of ourselves....'

"There are weighty problems to be solved, there are vast improvements yet to be made.... But Little Dover has a plan."

Other articles in Brown's newspaper series talked about the birth of a fledgling textile industry in Canso, with Sisters Denis Marie and Concepta teaching weaving classes. The looms are only one department. "During the day and evening women and girls operate spinning wheels to make yarn, knit and sew"—producing socks, mittens, woolen caps and other apparel. These nuns also administered the community library and reading room.

Flying out of Canso, Kingsley Brown ended one of the articles, "We could not help but feel that we had just seen unfolding in this remote and unexpected quarter of the globe a social experiment which writers a century hence may classify as historic."

Many years later, looking back, Brown told an

interviewer, "I didn't write too much about Tompkins [himself]. Everything Father Tompkins said at that time, in the context of the high feelings running about communism, would lead people to believe that he was a real radical, that he was hiding bombs in the glebe house."

AS WORD WENT OUT about co-ops and credit unions and study meetings—and Father Jimmy's letters and speeches were no small part of the broadcasts—more and more media as well as reformers discovered his parish. The showman in Tompkins wanted the local people to perform, to take pride in what they were accomplishing, and to tell the world. The impact of this outside interest and enthusiasm has yet to be calculated, but there were costs to guiding the visitors—and feeding them! The outcomes were both flattering and sometimes unflattering but always a time-consuming demand.

In 1935, Cecil Parker of Canso, one of the "little fellows," spoke for many others:

"Education very few of us possessed, and moreover many thought that Education was something a person got or did not get in his youth and that was the end of it. As for Organization, of course nearly everybody said you can't get the fishermen to stick together. About Cooperation, we knew very little. We often heard the word used by people who had no idea what the word meant. We were fortunate in our friends and some of them assured us that we were never too old to learn, that the time for learning anything was when you needed it. It did not take us long to discover that this was sound doctrine and practical as far as we were concerned."

The Catholic Church also seemed to be waking up. Archbishop Neil McNeil, a native of Nova Scotia, spoke at the opening of the Pontifical Institute of Medieval Studies at the University of Toronto in 1929. Father Jimmy secured a copy of the address in which McNeil mentioned the emphasis by the church in the Middle Ages on brotherhood and fellowship—"at once supernatural and supernational." The unity of the church had been shattered by the Reformation, making it little more than a piece of "spiritual machinery for saving the individual soul for another world...."

The social function of the church had been almost forgotten, claimed the archbishop. McNeil said that industrialization spawned an anti-church climate: "Now the fabric of industrialism seems to be crumbling by its own inherent rottenness and the cry for reconstruction is heard in all directions."

Marking up the address in red, Tompkins in Canso, who was doing what the hierarchy elsewhere hoped would happen, began a correspondence with the archbishop.

In 1935, echoing his earlier call in his column, "For the People" in *The Casket* in 1918, Tompkins sent out a clear message to Catholics everywhere:

"The Apostles went out without any apparently formulated economic doctrines but with tremendous convictions about the dignity of man, the worth of human personality and of the human soul. Before them political, social and economic kingdoms crumbled. If we in our day have a society that is pagan, is reeking with injustice, it is logical to expect that the same thing should happen now if we take our religion seriously. It seems to me that Christianity is the instrument that will do the job, provided there is real Christianity among us. We must today do more than talk platitudes and formulate metaphysical theories."

Three years later he lamented:

"It is not Christianity that is the opiate of the people, it is the inert state of Christians that furnished some semblance of truth to this libel. It is fossilized education that is the opiate of the people. It keeps them from getting the truth about the condition they are in...."

IN 1934, THE LITTLE PRIEST developed a sore throat, blaming it on the damp, fogbound climate of Canso. But he may well have sensed that it was time to leave this place. He needed new horizons, new audiences, new opportunities to spread the word of cooperation. Friends advised Father Jimmy that it might be time for a move. Dr. Learned of the Carnegie Foundation wrote:

"It is a heroic job you're doing, and I've often doubted whether even as a college president your example would have the influence which the great-hearted performance of your simple duties has on everyone who comes in contact with you. Still it seems to me that you cannot stay there long...."

Bishop Morrison sent Father Jimmy to be resident chaplain at Bethany, the Mother House of the Sisters of Saint Martha, set on a hill overlooking Antigonish. At a farewell celebration in Canso on Sunday, October 7, 1934, Father Poirier said of his friend and mentor:

"He proved without doubt that he is a man of God and a man of the people. He was a missionary in the full sense of the word. He wished to see God operate in every field of human activity. He wanted to make the universe praise God, with everything in it being used as divine aids helping men to attain everlasting life."

Father Jimmy had a comfortable life at Bethany, but he did not slow down. Attending chapel at 5:30 in the morning, he spent his day urging the sisters to engage in social action. He was not picky about his meals and easy to please. But George Boyle described him as "a wound-up alarm clock of God's love." He visited the Extension Department at St. Francis Xavier, home base of the Antigonish Movement, which was now working at high gear. Tompkins wrote:

"Every great teacher the world has ever seen went to the people, not so much to teach or inspire as to learn and to be inspired and encouraged to press on. The inspired teacher and the sympathetic listener mutually reacted upon each other and both became great.... St. Francis Xavier Extension Movement is mainly a gathering together, a sifting and a synthesis of the practical good sense, ideas and ideals of the common folk in the constituency of the University and a bringing back to them again their best thoughts in an orderly, organized and intensive manner through the various agencies (many of them voluntary) employed by the Extension Department."

MEANWHILE, FATHER JIMMY began to look around for new challenges. Conditions in the mining communities in Cape Breton, always deplorable, had become even worse. Exactly why Father Jimmy chose to go to Reserve Mines cannot be known. Key people in the Antigonish Movement, especially A. S. MacIntyre and M. J. MacKinnon, had put a great deal of effort into organizing workers in towns like Glace Bay and Reserve Mines. Was this heading off the rising interest in communism? The miners at Reserve Mines had shown initiative in starting their credit union on January 10, 1933.

Whatever the reason, the little priest gathered together his meagre possessions and on March 8, 1935, moved to Cape Breton to serve as parish priest at Reserve Mines.

CHAPTER FIVE

The Wise Man

"Dennis Coady just spent an hour or so in the house—the first time the bugger ever darkened the place or the church. He went away rejoicing with a copy of *Fire on the Earth*. He promises to take a course in reading from us."

Father Jimmy Tompkins

RESERVE MINES EXISTED for one reason—the rich coal deposits under the nearby land. The community lies thirteen kilometres east of Sydney, a short distance from Glace Bay on flat land close to the Atlantic Ocean. The name of the town derived from its designation as a "reserve" for the General Mining Association which had coal mines elsewhere in Nova Scotia. Mining began here in 1872, and by the time the new pastor arrived, the workings stretched far out under the ocean.

In the 'Thirties, pit head workings, colliery chimneys and spoil heaps dotted the landscape. Blackness marked the lives of the miners, from working in black pits and coming home with the coal dust still on them, to an education and religion surrounded by black-clad nuns and clergymen in black robes.

At the end of the nineteenth century, monopoly control of the coal industry had replaced frantic competition. Henry Melville Whitney, a Boston financier, took over collieries on the eastern side of Sydney Harbour, creating the Dominion Coal Company. To use the surplus coal from these workings, he founded the Dominion Iron and Steel Company. He sold out early, but by 1915 the company was producing 42% of Canada's coal. The profits did not stay in Cape Breton.

Hard times followed the First World War as the demand for coal and steel dropped. Faced with short-time and demands to cut their wages, the miners, between 1920 and 1925, went out on fifty-eight strikes in the Sydney coalfields. In February, 1925, the British Empire Steel and Coal Corporation (DOSCO had become BESCO), controlled by Roy "the Wolf" Wolvin, closed its mines at Reserve, Glace Bay, New Waterford and Sydney Mines, and cut off all credit at the company stores. The miners struck again, and a hungry, bitter year began in Reserve Mines. The strikers attacked, looted and burned the company-owned store.

In New Waterford a miner, Bill Davis, on his way home with milk for a new baby, was hit and killed by a stray bullet when company police fired on a protest march. Ottawa sent in the army in support of the civil power, claiming that anarchy threatened.

By July, 1925, the new Conservative provincial government of Edgar Rhodes intervened and secured compromises between the United Mine Workers and BESCO. The premier himself went to Sydney to negotiate a settlement. Wages would be cut by six to eight per cent and the company offered a rebate of one-fifth of the provincial coal royalties. And a government enquiry would examine the industry. The miners voted to return to work, and the company began to reopen the pits.

BESCO lost $1.5 million in coal sales; the miners—500 of whom found themselves blacklisted—lost $7 million in wages. The company never reopened their stores.

Sir Andrew Rae Duncan, chairman of the advisory committee to the British Department of Mines, a Scot, headed the provincial enquiry, on which also sat Rev. Dr. H.R. MacPherson, president of St. F. X., and Major Hume Cronyn, a prominent Tory businessman from Ontario.

The Duncan Commission heard a great deal about the miserable living conditions of coal miners and the deplorable state of company houses. Built between 1895 and 1910, these dwellings contained "two up and two down"—four rooms in all. Cramped, cold, damp, lacking basements and running water, heated by a kitchen stove and a fireplace in the parlour that let in more draft than it gave out in heat, the houses were insulated with cardboard against the winter blasts.

The Duncan Commission reported:

"There is much complaint of the leaky condition of the roofs, of ill-fitting doors and windows, of floors that are rotted or badly worn and of walls on which paper and plaster are in shreds and patches.... The badly rutted streets, the straggling fences, and the outside privies add to the unattractiveness of the general picture."

A miner told Father Jimmy, "If I dropped seed on the floors, they'd go down in the cracks and in the spring they'd sprout up through the floor."

A doctor told the commission of the high infant mortality in Glace Bay; two people had died of typhoid in New Waterford since the strike. The commission suggested that the provincial government do something about conditions in the mining towns, and that BESCO get rid of its houses.

BITTER MEMORIES OF THE 1925 STRIKE still pervaded Reserve Mines when the new priest arrived ten years later. In contrast to the highly independent ways of inshore fishermen, coal miners in Cape Breton had developed strong bonds of community and brotherhood. Strikes strengthened their sense of unity, and unions taught them the rudiments of organization, agitation and presentation to government. But, dominated by absentee owners and an American-based union, they had little control over their own lives. The miners lived by the colliery whistle. One blast meant work, two meant another idle day. If the miners worked two days, that was a good week. One more shift and there would be butter on the potatoes and meat with the bread.

Mary Ellicott Arnold, who became Father Jimmy's staunch ally in Reserve, described the town:

"Reserve Mines is not so very different from other little mining towns. There is a narrow main street, rutty in spring and icy in winter. There are rows of company houses. There is smoke from No. 10 that drifts in a long streamer across the town. There is life regimented by the whistles. In 1937 and 1938 there was a problem of feeding a family from a pay envelope which held only pay from three days work in the mine. But there was also something different which makes Reserve very different indeed from other mining towns. There is the Glebe House and Dr. Tompkins."

Father Coady pointed out:

"[Father Tompkins] could adjust himself to his environment whatever it might be.... He was, as a parish priest, a solicitous spiritual leader. But also, in the fishing community of Canso, he was a fisherman directly concerned with the economic and social problems of the community.... In Reserve Mines, he was a miner; the vicissitudes of his parishioners were his as well as theirs, and they were many...."

Mary and Joe Laben, local people, worked closely with the new priest. Mary observed:

"Dr. Tompkins came to Reserve in 1935. And of course the first thing that he did, he gave one look around and saw everybody standing around the corners and going to taverns and everything else, and I guess he said, 'I guess I better start doing something.' So he got a library. Organized with the help of the Carnegie Foundation, you know. He'd pinhole every boy or girl that he'd meet on the street to go to the library to read. So Joe went to the library with Father Jimmy and he started reading his books."

The priest's church, St. Joseph's, stood at the opposite end of the town from the colliery, and had a congregation of four hundred families. Father Jimmy settled quickly into his pastoral duties, counseling parishioners and taking night calls when mine accidents occurred. He kept a stack of books and papers by the side of his bed, and read as voraciously as ever. His curate, Father Allan MacAdam, often met him in the rectory corridor at six in the morning. "Say, Mac, have you seen this?" the old priest would ask, thrusting forward a book with sections underlined and fierce scrawls in the margins.

A friend of Father Jimmy's sent him some adult education material in 1936, writing, "I marvel at your unlimited energy. Where you go, things happen."

In the pulpit, the priest devoted his sermons to local issues. Joe Laben held book Number 4 in the credit union he helped establish in Reserve Mines. He had gone to study meetings held by Fr. Coady and A. B. MacDonald. A highly intelligent man with a photographic memory and a Grade 3 education, Joe recalled:

"Prior to Dr. Jimmy, we were scared of priests. We had some very cross priests that would never bother with the people at all. They would give them hell and preach brimstone and the devil and a lot of superstitious stuff. We were so inferior and afraid. They preached fear of God rather than love of God—how God loves us and when we work and do things for each other, that can be an act of prayer. That's the kind of religion Dr. Jimmy spoke.

"He told us this story about a community—they all woke up in the morning and their elbows were fused. And they sat down for breakfast and they filled their spoon and the food would go right over their heads. They did not know what to do about it. So they called in the wise man. He sized up the situation and said, 'Try feeding the fellow across from you.' So he filled the plate and fed him and the guy across fed him—and that's how they were fed, helping one another.

"Dr. Jimmy taught that Christ was a very simple person. He was a revolutionist. He wanted change."

Many years later, Mary Laben told how Father Jimmy nurtured potential community leaders:

"Father Jimmy was an individualist. He pinpointed you. He picked out Jimmy Marsh and he picked out Joe. He concentrated and made sure that they read the things they were supposed to."

Jimmy Marsh recalled Father Jimmy's influence:

"We didn't know if we were communists or

Catholics. We heard the communists and they used to rile us up, singing the 'Red Flag' and going to meetings at midnight—we thought it was great. We were just young, open to ideas; maybe we were being developed in the wrong way....

"[Father Jimmy] certainly changed my life. I was a fly-by-night young fellow.... And when he came around here first, we didn't know anything about education. All we thought about when we were young was to get a job in the pit. There was no mention of any kind of reform. Things were pretty bleak. And he made us realize what was going on. He said we needed education and a system of self-help.... He started telling us, 'You've got to do something about your system. The rich are getting richer and the poor getting poorer. The first thing you people want to do is start reading books about everything—especially economics....'"

Every Saturday, whatever the weather, Father Jimmy walked or cycled up to the Laben house. Mary gave him a glass of milk and a tea biscuit, and soon "he was talking at the same time he was eating." Joe, working in the pit until eleven at night, would just settle in bed when the phone would ring. It was Father Jimmy. As Mary Laben put it: "He read things to Joe on the phone every blessed night."

"I wasn't around at the time," recalled Sister Francis Dolores, "but when he came [to Reserve] he looked around and he said to himself that what was needed here was some kind of educational backup.

They were having those night schools over there by the Junior, in the basement of the school. And he said, 'They need books, they need books, they need more than handouts or pamphlets,' and he started running down the Extension movement. 'Handouts,' he used to say, 'from Coady's pocket, isn't enough.' And it sounded derogatory at the time but he was getting a point across."

ONE DAY, AFTER HE HAD FIRST put out his own books in the vestibule of the rectory, he decided to start a real library. Clearing the front room of the glebe house of furniture, he installed shelves and filled them with books, creating the first "People's Library." Buttonholing individuals on the street, Father Jimmy would say, "Come to the glebe house and I'll get you any book you need. The man who reads is the man who leads."

Father Jimmy saw books—the right kinds of books—as a way of preparing people for social and economic action. He saw the library as a powerhouse, and recognized the vital role of the librarian in social change. He later wrote: "The trained librarian of the Regional Library ought to be, first and foremost, an Adult Educator. It is one thing to be active in the library service and it may be quite another thing to be a promoter of Adult Education. Adult Education works towards the development of the community. A library might unwittingly become a hindrance rather than a help in the spread of genuine education—Adult or otherwise—and becomes like so much formal education in the past, the opiate of the people."

Father Jimmy's glebe house library opened on July 5, 1935, four months after he arrived in the parish. The room blossomed with slogans, clippings from the priest's readings, books, banners and papers of all kinds. Children discovered its wonders, and took home books, arousing the interest of their parents. The library filled up on Saturday nights, and people from outside the parish came to read and borrow books. The collection numbered around 2,000 volumes, with about a tenth of them in circulation each week. Father Jimmy suggested that people read Marx—and his own particular favourite, J.P. Warbasse's *Cooperative Democracy*. He also recommended *Up from Slavery* by Booker T. Washington, the Black American educator, to inspire the oppressed miners.

J. King Gordon told of his visit to the library soon after it opened:

"We made our way to the presbytery of Father James Tompkins. On the verandah was a notice board telling of the doings of the Associated Study Clubs and Credit Union of Reserve. In the centre of the board was a flaming square of red—the cover of *Social Planning for Canada* blazing out its message to the passersby on the street.

"James Tompkins met us at the door. He is a small man with deep set clear blue eyes. His is a face which you do not forget—the face of a zealot, a prophet, a fanatic perhaps—the face of a man in

126

whose vocabulary the word 'defeat' finds no place....

"We entered his library which was converted into the public library of the village. Well catalogued, administered by a competent librarian...."

Gordon caught the essence of his host as he wrote about a conversation that soon became a typical Father Jimmy monologue:

"Have you read Agar's *Land of the Free?*

"A stimulating thing; you should read it.

"These pamphlets are good; show a new technique in presenting social and economic facts.

"What did you say was the name of the book you think we should have? Much used?

"It's amazing: I know of two miners who walked eight miles to borrow books.

"They are all reading."

Father Jimmy had an eclectic view of the sort of literature people needed to make sense of the world: "You can get books on any imaginable topic.... Books create a centre of interest, study and discussion. The people can't do this job of self-help unless they are stimulated. They've got to have the information, too, and the motives. They've got to want to be something."

He also recognized that people needed a guide in the vast world of books he was acquiring: "A library is not only books. A library is books plus a trained librarian."

WITH INCREASED DEMANDS on the library in

Reserve Mines, Father Jimmy cast around for a librarian to run it. He asked the Sisters of Charity for one, only to be told that they were teachers—not librarians. So the priest threatened to go to the Sisters of Saint Martha for the person he needed. The Sisters of Charity relented and sent Sister Francis Dolores, who had just taken a degree in Librarianship.

"Much against my will and total dismay in fact, I was told I was lent out to a man named Dr. Jimmy Tompkins who lived in Reserve—wherever that was."

Sister Francis Dolores thought the town would be "the extreme of desolation." She arrived in Reserve in September, 1940.

"I [had] thought I was going to be a professor [at Mount Saint Vincent University] and here I was being shoved off to the backwoods, wherever the backwoods was. And I got down there and within a year I'm saying to myself, 'This is what I was looking for all my life.' Stimulation. Exciting opportunity for growth, a oneness with a friend, people who are there waiting to be drawn out, young people. And the year went by and went into ten—and the ten years went. I can't believe I spent a decade there.... I wasn't there a month and it was like chemistry. Dr. Jimmy and I were just merging into each other's philosophy and I was clicking. I knew I was in a place where I was going to live and grow....

"He had this small library created in the front room of the rectory...and he was keeping it alive from funds from the Credit Union and the Co-op store and the odd donation. I suppose some from himself. But he had all of the new books and he was particularly interested in the TVA [Tennessee Valley Authority] and economic books. And...good fiction....

"And we had marvelous little discussion groups that he would sit in on...and it was during the war years and we had a lot of talk about [that] and we had all the war books...when they came out from those war correspondents. And the boys were reading them and discussing them. And he'd come in and listen and he was putting his foot on the chair, you know, listening. He was tremendously impressed with it....

"So very often we'd have some celebrity...the Deputy Minister of the Department of Agriculture in Washington would come up with his team. The Lorimers—they were Russian experts. People like that would come and he'd ask them to stay overnight. And they'd get those young people over talking and people would be just entranced listening to those young people talking about books they had read. And even the kids, he'd get the kids to say, 'What book did you read this week?'...

"And so by 1945, he was convinced that what we had to have was a supportive school library and what did he do he cleaned out that whole basement [of St. Joseph's school] and he put in that very attractive school library area."

"And he got me on the public payroll of the

Cape Breton school system as a paid librarian. I guess I was the first librarian in Nova Scotia history to be paid a salary [as a] full-time school librarian. So I would do that during the day and in the evenings I would go to the People's School library and work with the adults."

The library had spoken books on records and children would sit around the phonograph listening to Dickens and Browning. Father Jimmy wanted beautiful, illustrated books for children to excite them and hook them on reading. Sister Francis Dolores:

"And then he'd get them to talk about it afterwards. We put in an awful lot of garden books...and everybody began to read gardens."

He encouraged a group of miners to acquire some land and start farming it. Mary Laben remembered:

"The mines were only working two days a week and he wanted people to be able to feed themselves. He got affiliated with the Agricultural College in Truro. He got an ag. representative sent in here, in fact he got two of them. One was Lynton Martin and the other was Fred Proudfoot. They went around to meetings. Everybody started from scratch. They started ploughing the land. They rented a tractor first and eventually they bought it."

This gardens project prospered. Nearly seventy-five families participated, encouraged by Father Leo Sears who came as curate in September, 1941. George Boyle noted that "they had ninety acres under cultivation in the back yards. They had a co-operative brooder for chickens."

Mary Laben tells how it was done:

"We all had study clubs. We all made our own quilts. We had two people from Truro who came down and showed us how to can everything in our garden that could be canned. We had our own cannery. One winter I had 1,300 cans—peas, beans, strawberries and everything else. You look back at it and wonder who did it!

"It was friendly. People visited and talked of their troubles. If you could help you were doing it, you know."

The miners and their wives could do little about the major forces in the company-dominated community. But they could start taking actions to better their lives, urged on by their priests.

RESERVE MINES BECAME a centre for learning and a place of pilgrimage for those seeking to help others create a better life. Mary Arnold wrote about the climate for action created by Father Jimmy:

"Those who study at the 'University of Reserve Mines' are not always aware that they are at a university nor how much they are learning. There is talk with Dr. Tompkins in his crowded little library where letters and books and papers from all over the world lie scattered on desks and tables and chairs, and even on the floor after the mail has just come in."

Mary Laben said there was "talk of a store...of

fish plants and one thing and another." Study clubs flourished in the community, while Father Jimmy kept up the pressure to initiate a system of regional libraries. He spoke to school trustees:

"A library is not an invention to kill time, but is a place to get information on subjects in which we are interested.... There are clever and vital people in every community and it is extremely important that such people be intellectually fed, because it means everything to the community.... Education should take hold of people where they are and enable them to develop along their own lines.... We are beginning to understand the great possibility of books and the corresponding responsibility of the State and general public to provide a reading service for all....

"We need a general awakening in Canada on the important matter of library service, and we might well adopt the motto in this day and age: 'Books for Everybody.'"

And again:

"I want regional libraries because I want the people to be able to know a fool when they see one."

IN 1937, THE PROVINCIAL GOVERNMENT had passed the Regional Libraries Act, which allowed municipalities to vote tax money for their establishment. Nora Bateson, a pioneer librarian who, with the help of a Carnegie grant, had started a library system from scratch in British Columbia's

Fraser Valley in 1930, was invited to survey libraries in Nova Scotia. Bateson's report had harsh words about the state of libraries in the province and urged the establishment of a regional system. Under her direction, Cape Breton was selected as a site for a regional library in 1938. She helped Father Jimmy publish a pamphlet, "Why not a Cooperative Library?" Despite her energy and Father Jimmy's enthusiasm, this venture failed because the towns were in debt, unemployment was high, and municipal services cut to the bone.

In 1940, the Carnegie Corporation offered the Nova Scotia Regional Libraries Commission $50,000 for the purchase of books, to be matched by the provincial government over a five-year period. Only the first $10,000 ever arrived. The Second World War diverted interest away from libraries.

Sister Francis Dolores recalled:

"When the war broke out the government drew the blinds down on any talk about a Regional Library system and put all the money they had into war-time libraries [for service people] in Halifax."

Nora Bateson's energies went into the Canadian Legion War Services Library; she would go on to be director of libraries for Nova Scotia.

Sister Dolores described how Father Jimmy kept the idea of regional libraries alive: "[Father Tompkins] didn't stop talking. He still kept that thing alive.... During the war...they'd put these very glossy ads in *Time* magazine and *Newsweek*—these big corporations would, like Ford—to say, 'We're still in business. When the lights go up again we'll be making Fords'—so you wouldn't forget the name of Ford.... And Jimmy was doing the same thing, he was talking up a storm about the Regional Library."

In June, 1941, Father Jimmy had to be in Boston to receive an honorary degree from Harvard. He had also been invited to address the Maritime Library Association on the same day. "I can't be in both places," he told Sister Dolores, "so I'm going to tell them you are to take my place." Sister Dolores protested. What would *she* talk about? And she had to secure the permission of her order to give a speech. Father Jimmy told her that he'd square things with her superior in Halifax. As her topic she should talk about what was happening right there in Reserve Mines. "That's a story for anyone."

It was a good example of Father Jimmy's very direct style.

"When he was pushing at things," Sister Dolores said, "he pushed too hard. He always pushed too hard—he made people feel they didn't know anything. When he was telling these curates [and other people, that they] should be reading something, he doesn't say, 'You should be reading something.' He'd say, 'You big fatheads'—you know—'it's time you started to learn something.'" Encouraging people to read and think was "the kind of task that he felt he had to do and it was always eating away at him. He wasn't fulfilled."

Tompkins pushed all the time, everywhere.

Even at confession. It is said that he would skirt the sins and ask his parishioners what was the last book they had read. He had once said:

"The man who has not read a book in the past year is not fit to walk the streets of a democracy."

Out of it all, Mary Laben said that ordinary people began to study and understand their world:

"In Reserve they had organized twenty-three study clubs, meeting in people's houses. So every Sunday evening after Mass there'd be nine or ten or eleven arrive at my little house in Belgium Town. And I'd go to another house where there was a bunch of women holding a meeting.... They had a question box, and everybody was asked to put a question in the box...and if they couldn't answer it among themselves they got Dr. T. to answer it."

The credit union in Reserve flourished. Under Father Jimmy's prodding a group of miners opened their own cooperative store in 1937. Word of the priest's achievements spread across North America. Reserve Mines became an important stop on tours organized by American social activists and reformers. Rev. James E. Byrnes, Secretary of the National Catholic Life Conference, called the People's Library, "The 'University of Reserve Mines.' The buildings weren't much, but what a man is Tompkins, the Chancellor, President and Faculty."

Tompkins visited Antigonish in the years before the Second World War to take part in the Rural and Industrial Conferences. In a speech in August, 1938, he said:

"Adult education is not for illiterates alone nor is it to pap-feed social climbers with appreciation of Shakespeare and Beethoven. It should be designed for the best brains we have to wrestle with the worst problems we have....

"People in times of crisis have to be shocked into knowing the true nature of things. People have, for too long, been fooled into hiding their light under a bushel, largely by propaganda for laissez faire and in the interests of the great...."

For Tompkins, religion, language, gender did not matter at the grassroots. Whatever was achieved there in making a better life becomes "the possession of all, like a scientific discovery." The local Protestant minister sat with him on the rectory verandah, something that had never happened before.

"When I was growing up," Mary Laben said, "you wouldn't dare look at the side of the road that the [other] church was on. Father Jimmy changed that."

And one of his achievements literally put Father Jimmy—and his name—on the map of Canada.

CHAPTER SIX

A Name on the Map

"We didn't realize we could lead."
Jimmy Marsh

IN HIS INTRODUCTION to Mary Arnold's book, *The Story of Tompkinsville*, Father Coady recalled receiving "a bit of a shock...."

The first study club he'd helped to organize, the one in Reserve Mines, came to the conclusion that they wanted to study cooperative housing—and build their own houses. The March, 1934, issue of St. F.X.'s Extension Department bulletin had urged people to study housing. The idea for the first cooperative housing venture in Nova Scotia took shape with the study club meeting in Mary Laben's kitchen—when a question drawn from the box asked: "Why can't we build our own homes?"

Everyone laughed at the idea.

But when they mentioned the question to Father Jimmy, he asked, "Why can't you?" He reminded them of their reading in J. P. Warbasse's *Cooperative Democracy*, pointing out that the rents charged for their miserable company houses were enough to pay for them every twenty years. "Then you turn around and give the houses to the coal company. If you're that rich, why don't you build your own houses?"

With that, the "shocked" Father Coady had to deal with a demand from miners in Reserve seeking to move from talk to action.

Father Jimmy went to Halifax and discovered that the Nova Scotia government had passed an act in 1932 offering loans "to assist in providing dwellings for families with an income of $1,200 or less per year and who consequently cannot afford to pay more than fifteen or twenty dollars a month as rent or in the way of monthly installments to enable them to purchase a home over a period of 20 years."

The Nova Scotia Housing Commission could put up 75% of the cost of appraised value of the house in the form of a long-term, low-interest loan. The act, the first of its kind in Canada, resulted from the efforts of Rev. Dr. Samuel Prince. Known as "Sammy the Prince," this innovative, activist Anglican priest, a professor of sociology at King's College in Halifax, served as a member of the Provincial Housing Commission. The housing act required that potential homeowners put up 25% of the costs of land acquisition and construction, for a total of $500. In 1937, annual earnings of men at Dominion Coal Company averaged $1,263. In the following year, it dropped to $1,069, rising to $1,211 in 1939.

What hope did miners working only a couple of shifts a week have of owning their own homes? The idea appeared absurd. But the study group kept considering the possibility.

As Mary Laben put it, Father Jimmy kept the idea alive by getting the act changed to read "land and labour"—instead of $500 in cash. If the miners put up $100, the other $400 could come from sweat equity—if they built their own homes. But the study club kept stumbling on the fundamental problem. None of its members—or Father Jimmy or anyone else—knew anything about the practice of building cooperative housing.

IN 1937 JOE LABEN, the leader of the group, gave a paper on the concept at the annual St. F.X. Conference in Antigonish. These events drew people from all over the world; *The Times* of London and *The New York Times* sent reporters to cover them. Mary Arnold and her longtime companion Mabel Reed came to the 1937 conference, sponsored by the Co-op League in the United States. The two had reached a crisis back home.

Of Mabel Reed, nothing much is known. But Mary Arnold was a woman way ahead of her time, highly intelligent, able, socially committed, with an oddly checkered background. Daughter of a New York financier ruined in the crash of 1873, her weak heart and poor eyesight prevented her from attending school. She educated herself with the help of her father's books, learning all of Shakespeare's plays by heart. Before the First World War, she worked as an Indian agent in California and took courses in dietetics at the University of California and Cornell University. During the war, she worked in a plant making torpedoes, hiring and training women to replace men who had entered the armed forces.

Then in 1919 Mary Arnold started the 25th Street Co-operative Cafeteria in New York. It grew into the Consumers' Co-operative Society with eight branches, its own bakery and four thousand members. Arnold had studied cooperatives in Europe and North America, serving as treasurer of the Co-operative League of the United States from 1924 to 1937.

But the cooperative venture she managed in New York was in trouble. As she put it in a letter:

"An unpopular communist union was demanding recognition from an unwilling membership and equally unwilling workers. At all points we were torn apart by divided loyalties. Under the strain and over the period of a year, all our attempts at education proved inadequate.

"We felt the need of a new vision and a new understanding. We were to find that vision and understanding in Nova Scotia. We were also to find two of the greatest men we have ever known: Father Coady and Father Jimmy Tompkins."

When Father Coady discovered the experience the two women had in cooperative housing—Mary Arnold's consumers' co-op in New York had erected a sixty-seven-unit apartment building—he suggested they travel to Cape Breton.

"We introduced Miss Arnold to our troublesome group of miners at Reserve and sat back with a feeling of intense relief."

Arnold and Reed intended to spend only a day with Father Jimmy. Listening to him, Arnold recalled, "he began to make us see something else. Something we had missed in eighteen years in a cooperative in New York City. A belief in people. The power that is in all of us to help ourselves." The priest told the two women about the Reserve Mines study group on cooperative housing—"But they don't know how to go about it." Would the ladies like to meet the men? Father Jimmy made a phone call. "It's all fixed up."

Instead of returning to the United States, Mary Arnold and Mabel Reed spent two years at the "University of Reserve Mines"—"sitting at the feet of Father Jimmy Tompkins."

THE NEW AMENDED HOUSING ACT made it possible for working people to own their own homes in Nova Scotia—if they knew how to go about building them. Mary Arnold later wrote that the legislation made the task seem achievable, and that was the reason she decided to stay in Cape Breton. Then Arnold, in turn, convinced the Nova Scotia Housing Commission that the 1932 Act could be further amended to apply to cooperative ventures.

The miners and their wives had spent a lot of

time discussing building their own houses. Mary Arnold and Mabel Reed, inspired by Father Jimmy—and obviously somewhat burned-out by the conflicts in their New York venture—found a new focus for their energy and idealism, providing the technical and organizational skills. Arnold shared Father Jimmy's unique ability to plunge into a situation and start things moving.

In October, 1937, the miners, with their wives and families, looked over a piece of land owned by the parish. It had been designated for expansion of the cemetery. If each of the ten members of the housing club could pay $50, Father Jimmy would sell them a ten-acre parcel:

"Yes, it would make a nice resting place for the dead. But I think we should let the living have it right now."

Mary Arnold organized study sessions over a 26-week period. Details of construction had to be worked out. Mary Laben recalled that the wives had a large say in how the houses were planned:

"The women...all built little cardboard homes.... Katie McNabb, she did her whole kitchen around because she had eight [children].... She put a window in the middle on both sides. She put whole cupboards [in] because she'd need them... and then room for her table and room for her stove and that went into her kitchen."

Sixty years later, the excitement and tensions still run through Mary Arnold's book about building the cooperative housing development. The houses would be built to a standard form of exterior construction. But while it was hard to tell one company house from the other—"If you are a comparative stranger in Reserve and wish to visit a friend, you take the nearest telegraph pole and count down from it two, three or four houses as the case may be. All the [company] houses are painted dark green or brown"—each new home built by the study club would have individual touches, inside and out.

To estimate the costs of construction, a "budget house" was built for Mary Arnold and Mabel Reed. It cost $2,500. If members of the group provided land and labour, the cost could be kept to less than $2,000. The Labens and others kept detailed accounts of costs in five-cent scribblers. The Laben house cost $1,048, with the principal, interest, taxes and insurance coming to $7.47 a month.

Later, $2.50 was added to the monthly fee to create a reserve fund—"put in every month so that if anything happened like a windstorm or anything and one of those houses got the shingles blown off or anything, we had the money in the reserve fund to replace it."

One source of delight came when the budget house, built by a private contractor, proved to be the only one that leaked when the project was completed.

The women began to make things for their new houses. Mary Laben recalled:

"Somebody the government sent down from Truro...taught us with a loom to weave. We did quite a bit of that, and we knit and crocheted."

In March, 1938, the Arnold Cooperative Housing Association Ltd. came into being, with its capital of $24,000 divided into 4,800 shares valued at five dollars each. The eleven members of the housing club—one member's family would move into the budget house when the two women left—served as the Board of Directors.

A photograph recorded the birth of this unique cooperative venture, the first of its kind in North America. Mary Arnold described the scene in her book:

"'Now don't move,' said Dan MacNeil, 'until I get this picture. This camera doesn't seem to be acting just right.' Everyone sat rigid. 'There,' said Dan.

"This group of landless proletariat had become owners of eleven acres of land, worth $500. They sat back, and drew a long breath. Then every man turned to the little priest in their midst, and spoke the words upon which all had agreed: 'It is to be called Tompkinsville.'"

Their words came as a complete surprise to Father Jimmy.

TOMPKINSVILLE did not come into being without tensions and disappointments. Over the winter of 1937-38, the miners scraped together the money to pay for the lots. The loan from the housing commission did not arrive as they prepared to start building their new homes. Their ownership would be vested in the cooperative not the individual, an idea that generated derision among other miners: "Do you mean that a man does not own his own home? Gosh, that's a crazy idea. You can't make that work."

This skepticism strengthened the sense of community in the group as the frost came out of the ground. John Allen Smith declared that, loan or no loan, he was going to dig the foundation of his house. Others followed suit. Finally, the cheque arrived.

Foundations were poured—two a day, despite a defective concrete mixer. Then work slowed down, and a board meeting exploded in arguments and grudges. The group reorganized, with Duncan Currie elected foreman and a schedule of hours worked and tasks to be done drawn up. A carpenter was hired to advise the miners. A son and his friend worked on the house while one father was on a shift. "This house is just as much yours as it is mine," one father had told his twelve-year old.

And the women often worked alongside the men on the construction. Mary Laben:

"There's more shingles went on those houses with women than there were with men. They helped to put up the gyprock and everything....

"The day we moved in here was November the 27th, 1938—and we came in first so the Eastern Light and Power Company would connect the lights—they wouldn't do it till there was somebody in—so the rest of the men could work in the evenings by lamp[light]. The day that I came in we had to wait for them to put down the floor to put the stove up....

"And I knew we were moving—it was slushy—it was the 27th of November—so day before I made a great big pot of stew and a pile of homemade bread. And all the men were working here 'cause they knew we were moving in, to get the floor down. They had two wooden horses and they put a sheet of gyprock on it and put the stew in the middle of it and passed the plates all around and everybody had the first meal on a sheet of gyprock—homemade stew and apple pie and homemade bread."

And Joe added: "And we got a bottle of moonshine."

Tompkinsville formally opened on August 13, 1938, marked by a large ceremony. Five hundred people attended, including 150 participants of a tour organized by the Co-operative League of the U.S.A. Premier Angus L. MacDonald, a friend of Father Jimmy's for many years, put great stress in his address on "right thinking" because "subversive agencies" were at work in Nova Scotia. A report on the event stated:

"The custom of looking to governments, Premier MacDonald said, may have grown to undue proportions and it was good to see people, such as those ten miners whose houses in various stages of completion surrounded the speaker, return to the spirit of their forefathers and provide homes by their own hard work."

Sammy the Prince also spoke, foreseeing beauty spots emerging from the drabness of the mining village. He, too, extolled the miners whose "divine discontent had transformed a distant hope into a reality." The cooperative movement, he declared, "had come into this province like a rainbow of hope in dark skies." It had made Tompkinsville possible.

MUCH REMAINED TO BE DONE as the days grew colder, the nights longer. Water pipes went in as the men worked frantically to beat the winter. Ed Kelly's house was the last one to be finished. They put in the final pipe on the project the day before winter struck and the ground went rock hard. "But let her come," said the men, as they turned to the inside work. The families moved into their new homes. As Mary Laben put it: "All you've got to have is a stove and a bed and a table." With Joe, she pushed a final cart loaded with possessions through the cold rain to the new house. Nine families celebrated Christmas in Tompkinsville.

And Mary Arnold wrote *The Story of Tompkinsville*, published by the Co-operative League of New York, in 1940. It attracted attention all over North America. Soon visitors came to see what ordinary men and women had done through cooperation. Mary Arnold played down her role and that of Mabel Reed. As she put it, "Cooperation may go slowly but it goes safely."

A reporter expressed surprise at what the miners had achieved, "They aren't just workingmen's

houses, but houses anyone might care to live in."
Each had six rooms and a bath, copper plumbing,
open and spacious living and dining rooms and
"charming and gay" kitchens, planned by the wom-
en "for the greatest possible efficiency."

Travel writer Clara Dennis, visiting Cape Breton in 1938, gushed:

"There were the most adorable little kitchens
in the houses...kitchens that would delight the
heart of any housewife. To the miner's wife they
were a special joy for with the different shifts in the
mine, she might have to prepare as many as seven
or eight different meals a day instead of the regular
three.... One kitchen was red and gray, with red and
gray linoleum on the floor. Another had black linoleum and the chairs were Spanish red and Royal
blue...."

One member of the housing group told Father
Jimmy, "I learned more in the last year than I did in
the other twenty-seven of my life."

YEARS LATER, at the burning of the mortgages for
the houses, the celebrants sang a song composed by
Agnes and Eddie Gallant to the tune of "The Battle
Hymn of the Republic."

Hurrah to Tompkinsville!!

Mary Arnold came to town to see what she could do
Along with Doctor Jimmy and Doctor Coady too.
They all got together, to help the working man
To build a home of his own.

The chorus went:

> Come and let us sing together,
> Come and let us sing together
> Come and let us sing together,
> Hurrah to Tompkinsville!

The song captures, in six verses, the spirit, energy and enthusiasm that Father Jimmy had generated in this small group of men and women, and which Mary Arnold and Mabel Reed had harnessed and directed into an innovative venture that no one else in North America had ever attempted.

"When we paid back for those houses," Mary Laben remembered, "we paid back $7.47 a month—and that was as hard for us to do on two shifts with the families that were here as what it is today for a family to pay $300.00...."

EVEN BEFORE THEIR OWNERS had moved into Tompkinsville, study groups formed in Dominion and Sterling to discuss cooperative housing. By 1940 they had begun to build Villa Nova and Reedville. Joe Laben, after twenty-five years as a miner—his last pay packet in 1941 contained one cent, and long after he died Mary still treasured the pay envelope—joined the Sydney office of St. F.X.'s Extension Department and began to spread the gospel of co-op housing, traveling to Prince Edward Island and, at the invitation of Premier Smallwood, to Newfoundland.

In time, Laben would write one of the best

handbooks on cooperative housing, and inspire others to follow the path that he and his friends had taken in a time of despair and depression. Rev. J.D. Nelson MacDonald, a United Church minister from Cape Breton, had been recruited as a part-time extension worker by Father Coady in 1936. He moved to Dartmouth on Nova Scotia's mainland in 1943, found people in dire need of housing, and called in Joe Laben to talk to the study clubs. Co-op housing ventures arose in Woodlawn. By 1953, the year of Father Jimmy's death, Nova Scotia had thirty-five housing cooperatives based on the Tompkinsville model. They had built four thousand homes.

Joe received the Order of Canada in 1984, and died the next year.

Although Tompkinsville represented a triumph of the cooperative spirit, and remains a beacon of light from a dark time in the history of Cape Breton, most miners and their wives and families continued to live in the squalid company houses. A survey of Reserve in 1945 identified 320 dwellings—half of them classified as shacks, and only twelve per cent of them with bathrooms. The worst conditions persisted near Tompkinsville.

IN THE MID-1940s, Father Jimmy began to fail. He would start a Mass service in church and then, halfway through, he would begin it again.

Father Coady had called him a "spark plug."

But now the spark no longer flashed.

CHAPTER SEVEN

The Dying Light

"I have not seen Dr. Tompkins since last Christmas, but I hear that he is getting weaker all the time."

Father Moses Coady

FATHER JIMMY HAD CONSIDERED writing a book in 1938 on the possibilities of adult education in resolving the social crisis. But he never started it, and his words are scattered throughout a wide range of articles, pamphlets, letters.

Articles appeared about him in *The Nation*, the *Montreal Standard*, the *Boston Advertiser*, *The New York Times* and *The Times* of London.

At an adult education conference in Niagara Falls, Bonaro Overstreet, an American writer, noticed a priest listening intently. She wrote in *Brave Enough for Life*, that "he leaned forward and spoke in quick, incisive phrases, about Nova Scotia and its cooperatives...." She recognized "Father Jimmy Tompkins, whose name is spoke with love and honor wherever adult educators or members of the cooperative movement talk of their job as one of building democracy from the ground up."

Until the mid-1940s, his mind seemed as sharp as ever.

In 1940, he received an unusual gift. Mrs. Andrew Carnegie sent him her late husband's coat, believing it should be worn by someone who shared his ideas. Tailored for the industrialist, lined with mink, the coat cost $10,000—and had been worn but once. So the radical priest warmed his last days with a garment crafted for a capitalist—until he became too frail to sustain its weight.

He became increasingly irascible, lashing out at Jimmy Marsh over the price of a piece of land on which to relocate the co-op store. "I thought you had brains, but I see I have been mistaken." Then he snapped off the light, leaving his friend in the dark with a lap full of pamphlets, grumbling, "I'm afraid there's nothing more I can do for you."

Father Jimmy argued openly with his curate who had planned the celebration of the 40th anniversary of his ordination in May, 1924. After listening to the tributes, Tompkins spoke out—if he merited all this fuss and if his ideas were sound, why didn't they follow them? Then Father Jimmy left the church.

He became increasingly forgetful.

But the old spirit flashed from time to time. In 1944, Sister Francis Dolores wrote from Halifax, suggesting using a room in the basement of the provincial technical school for evening classes in Reserve Mines. Back came a telegram the same day Father Jimmy received the letter:

"A capital idea. See the Department in Halifax about grants for school libraries." He pushed the idea and within a year the Young Peoples' Reading Room opened in the school.

He often sat in his library, a lonely figure waiting for visitors. In late November, 1946, the priest dictated a brief statement on "Books—the Franchises of the Mind" for the *Maritime Co-operator*, in which he defined charity as "helping people to help themselves."

In the summer of 1947, he wrote to Sister Dolores who was at the American Library Association Conference in California. Her address was, "Lone Mountain, San Francisco," and he remarked that his place was certainly "Lone Mountain, Reserve Mines."

Sister Dolores remembered: "I watched Dr. Tompkins mature, go to a pinnacle and start to subside. And I was there at his side when he was.... Away from the door, every five minutes he'd forget, he came home. 'I want the Sister'—you know? And just feeling that terrible helplessness that comes with knowing that you can't do a thing for a person that's disintegrating mentally...."

On July 2, 1948, at the age of 78, he had Sister Dolores prepare his letter of resignation as pastor of St. Joseph's—then he promptly forgot what he'd done and greeted the new pastor as a visitor.

Father Jimmy's cousin, Dr. Gregory Tompkins, came to examine him, and decided the priest needed full-time care. For unexplained reasons, he sent him to Saint Jean de Dieu Hospital in Montreal, run by French-speaking nuns, where he had to be restrained and tied down in his bed to prevent him from wandering. From Montreal, Father Jimmy wrote pathetic notes to another doctor friend, and he rescued him.

The Sisters of Charity at Margaree Forks built a special suite on to their convent and welcomed Father Jimmy home. He liked life here, looked after by a "MacNeil girl from Reserve."

But "he would roam on them," as Mary Laben put it. She and Joe came to visit him but Father Jimmy could not recognize the old miner. He did know who Mary was and, "My soul, was he ever glad to see me, he hugged me and hugged." Then he made tea for the visitors.

He still had "books and papers everywhere," Mary Laben recalled, and said he read every one of them. But he could remember nothing in them.

Father Jimmy loved the Saturday afternoon opera broadcasts and classical music, and flashes of his old wit appeared. Two nuns aided him for an outing, tying his shoelaces and brushing his jacket. "I must be a dandy," he remarked, "having two women looking after me."

A proposal to paint his portrait went to a committee who decided instead to raise funds to build a library to be named after him. Joe Laben headed the organization to carry through the idea, and the building in Margaree Forks opened on November 21, 1951. The credit union occupied half of it. But

Father Jimmy was not present. Two months earlier he had been moved to St. Mary's Hospital in Inverness. George Boyle visited him there, finding Father Jimmy staring and emaciated, fingers twisting the hem of his dressing gown. He recognized Boyle, who found him serene. But when the visitor told him that people wanted to hear the story of his life, Father Jimmy said, "There's nothing about me worth writing.... Too many duffers writing things nowadays...."

In 1952, the priest was moved again to St. Martha's Hospital in Antigonish. In that year, Father Coady wrote:

"Dr. Tompkins is by no means well. He was eighty-two yesterday. I don't go to see him anymore. I cannot bear visiting the man with the razor mind, the great inspirer, who is now reduced to a little bundle of ninety pounds of human flesh."

Father Jimmy Tompkins, spiritual father of the social action movement headed by his cousin, died on May 5, 1953.

His friends carried his coffin to the cemetery overlooking Tompkinsville and buried him there. One of these miners spoke words that resonated in the hearts and minds of all who knew him:

"By heaven, there was one hell of a man."

EPILOGUE

The Continuing Conversation

"I had always thought the sky to be our limit—which would not mean that we ought not to begin at the roots of things.... *Our* job is *fundamental*. All other sorts of development will follow. We are working at the grass roots."

Father Jimmy Tompkins

IN AUGUST 1985, the *Atlantic Co-operator* newspaper published a supplement about the annual Topshee Memorial Conference held at St. Francis Xavier University in Antigonish. It quoted Professor Dan MacInnes of the Sociology Department at St. F.X.:

"The focused vision and social critique of the once famed Antigonish Movement has virtually disappeared from public life. It has become that most dangerous of all Celtic mythic creatures—a live ghost. People closely associated with the movement pretend that things have worked out pretty well as had been planned."

MacInnes did not think that things had worked out as planned. And he suggested that if the people at that conference "should decide to...announce the death of the Antigonish Movement, we will be doing a service to those who constantly expect the Antigonish Movement to respond but hear silence.... The University and the Church should sign the death certificate. Since they gave the movement its birth, it is only fitting that they be made aware of its demise."

A journalist at the conference observed that Rev. Gregory MacKinnon, president of St. F.X., "didn't like what he was hearing.... MacInnes was butchering a sacred cow in the very cathedral where it had been baptized."

The image of the Antigonish Movement as a "live ghost" hung over the conference as participants debated the future of the co-operative movement and the fate of eastern Nova Scotia, the birthplace of the vital, energetic social action movement that changed the lives of so many of its people.

MacInnes asked:

"What has happened to the lofty ideals and organization efforts of fifty years ago? Were the fishermen in control or were the banks in control when they recently reorganized the Atlantic fishery? In the forest industry, who supervised the alleged rape of the woodlands over the last fifty years?... Is eastern Nova Scotia a monument to the success of the Antigonish Movement?"

Richard Cashin was also at the 1985 Topshee conference. He had attended St. F.X. during the 1940s at the height of the Coady era, and as president of the fishermen's union in Newfoundland, Cashin presided "over one of the youngest and most successful progeny of the Antigonish Movement." Only seven years after the conference, the federal government declared a moratorium on the overexploited cod stocks of Atlantic Canada, throwing 40,000 fisher folk out of work. TAGS— The Atlantic Groundfish Strategy—provided $1.9 billion over five years for these people to retrain or relocate. Most of the money, however, went into income support and kept people doing little or nothing in small fishing communities that had lost their economic base.

Father Jimmy's words echo down to our time: "If the government gives a man a $10 dole, he needs another as soon as it's gone. And he hasn't learned a damn thing, except how to stick out his hand."

But no one mentioned Father Jimmy's name at the 1985 conference, and the overall impression from the account in the *Atlantic Co-operator* was that the Antigonish Movement was simply an abstract idea. No flesh and blood and fallible humans created it, no breath of a particular spirit inspired and directed those who made it.

Had the conference participants forgotten their history?

THIS BOOK, *Father Jimmy*, is meant more as a tool

than as an answer for the economic and social problems of our time, more as a challenge and an inspiration to anyone today who is seeking ways to revitalize declining communities. Its aim has been to tell the story of the roots of the Antigonish Movement in terms of the life of its spiritual father, Father Jimmy Tompkins, and to keep alive the ideas and some of the earliest victories in cooperation in eastern Nova Scotia. In telling the story, we were struck again and again by the relevance of Father Jimmy's ideas and words for today.

This book is offered in the faith that ideas *can* have hands and feet, that they can live again and again, new every time in terms of the new circumstances. Otherwise, they *are* "fossilized education," the "opiate" Father Jimmy called them.

After the Great Crash of 1929, democratic governments in Europe and North America appeared to be paralyzed, doing little to assuage the misery caused by the depression that followed upon it. In Nova Scotia and elsewhere, small communities found themselves backed against a wall. Father Jimmy and his followers, using adult education techniques and fostering local democracy, showed people how to look over the wall—or knock a hole in it by their own efforts to make a better life for themselves.

SOME SAY THAT the Antigonish Movement is dead. They say that there is little difference between a co-op store and private supermarkets, between banks and credit unions—except that people can go to meetings. But in most cases they *don't* go, and door prizes are offered to lure members to meetings. As one 1985 Topshee participant said:

"Eighty percent of the members in my co-op aren't interested in cooperative philosophy. They are in it because it's a good buying club. Why try to build a social movement on the backs of people who aren't interested in social organizing?"

In the 1970s Joe Laben had said, "The mistake we made is that we didn't teach the young...."

And in a 1990s interview, Mary Laben lamented that even young people who had grown up in Tompkinsville did not know the story of the first housing cooperative in North America, achieved by their parents.

"Co-operation is spirit," Father Jimmy said, "not just passing pork and bologna over the counter to your neighbours." Some of the spirit of the early days of the Antigonish Movement comes through in a story told by Jim Charles MacNeil about a credit union in Cape Breton:

"A fellow took a loan to buy a delivery truck. Then that fellow became sick. So members of the credit union kept the truck going, made his deliveries. They made his monthly payments until the fellow was back on his feet. Saved his business. Saved the truck. Saved the credit union...."

Often, older cooperators explain the decline in initiative and participation by pointing to the coming of "good times," the money and transportation and wider opportunities brought in the wake of the Second World War. In Canada, they point to the government-administered security blanket that delivers health care and pensions.

The security blanket was certainly not in place in Father Jimmy's time, and he pointed out, again and again, that people could only save themselves by their own efforts. And today's security blanket is getting threadbare.

The co-ops and credit unions in Canada started among the "have-nots." Now they have become large, bureaucratized and comfortable, catering to the needs of the "haves." But their heritage and original dynamism is being continued by small groups of people on the margins of Canadian society. There should be no surprise in that. Tompkins did not set out to start a social movement. He simply wanted to make people more self-reliant. And he was always mistrustful of institutions and bureaucracy.

George Boyle wrote about an evening with Father Jimmy in the Reserve Mines parish house. The newspaper said that fire was threatening buildings of a university. Father Jimmy's reaction was that "it wouldn't hurt much if they were burnt out. Some of them should be burned down regularly every twenty-five years. It might bring them into contact with the people...."

So, is the Antigonish Movement dead? Perhaps the right question is whether the *spirit* of the Antigonish Movement is dead? The answer is part of the continuing conversation. It depends on our courage and capacity to deal with ideas anew, to give them hands and feet in the current realities. *That* seems to be the challenge, in Father Jimmy's time and in our own.

Jim Lotz
Michael R. Welton

ACKNOWLEDGEMENTS, SOURCES AND SUGGESTED READINGS

NO ONE CAN WRITE a biography of Father Jimmy Tompkins without acknowledging the work of his friend and first biographer, George Boyle. We also wish to thank Professor Sheldon Currie, Juanita M. MacDonald and Theresa MacNeil for a series of interviews with people who knew Father Jimmy. Kathleen MacKenzie, Archivist at St. Francis Xavier University, provided a great deal of help in sorting through the records there and providing ideas and direction for the book. We are also most grateful for the help of the staff at the Beaton Institute Archives at the University College of Cape Breton. Dr. Robert Morgan gave us his generous support and cooperation. We also appreciated the help of the staff at the Public Archives of Nova Scotia. Kingsley Brown, Jr., kindly provided copies of his father's writing and a letter from Father Jimmy. We would also like to thank Bonnie Thompson at Breton Books, and our publisher Ronald Caplan. His passionate concern for recovering and recording the history of Cape Breton proved to be a continual inspiration.

Both authors would like to express their appreciation for the support for their research from the Social Sciences and Humanities Research Council of Canada. Jim Lotz received a grant as a private scholar in 1989 to continue his work in community development, with special reference to the Antigonish Movement. Dr. Welton received support from the Council through its research support programme at Mount Saint Vincent University.

The research for this book was done mainly in three places in Nova Scotia. The main archival collection of Father Jimmy's papers rests in the Beaton Institute at the University College of Cape Breton. This holding includes correspondence with the Carnegie Corporation of New York, gathered by Father Greg MacLeod. The record of Father Jimmy's work at St. Francis Xavier University is held in its archives. The St. F.X. Extension papers contain numerous references to Father Jimmy, and a number of his significant letters to Father Coady, A.B. MacDonald and others. We also examined the wonderfully rich "Scrapbooks" of the Antigonish Movement, loyally and carefully kept by its activists. Very few researchers have made use of this rich source of material on a remarkable social action venture.

The Casket, the newspaper of the Diocese of Antigonish, contains much of interest to those who wish to learn more about Father Tompkins and his life and times. The Public Archives of Nova Scotia in Halifax has the transcripts of the Maclean Commission of 1927, and also a number of articles about Father Tompkins. This material helped us to catch the feel of the terrible years in the fisheries of the region, and provided perspectives on Father Tompkins from those who knew him. The Public Archives also has copies of the newspapers of his time, including the *Halifax Chronicle*, the *Halifax Herald*, *The Canso Breeze and Guysboro County Advocate*, the *Maritime Co-operator* and the St. F.X. *Extension Bulletin*.

Unfortunately, many of the books on Father Jimmy and the times in whch he lived are out of print or difficult to access. But there is increasing interest in the Antigonish Movement, and the following publications offer a valuable introduction to those great days when Nova Scotians sought to make a better life for themselves and their communities through their own efforts.

Alexander, Anne, *The Antigonish Movement: Moses Coady and Adult Education Today*. Toronto, Thompson Educational Publishing, 1997.

Arnold, Mary, *The Story of Tompkinsville*. New York, The Co-operative League, 1940.

Boyle, George, *Father Tompkins of Nova Scotia*. New York, P.J. Kennedy and Sons, 1953.

Cameron, James D., *For the People: A History of St. Francis Xavier University*. Montreal and Kingston, McGill-Queen's University Press, 1996.

Crerar, Duff, *Padres in No Man's Land: Canadian Chaplains and the Great War*. Montreal and Kingston, McGill-Queen's University Press, 1995.

"Father Jimmy Tompkins of Reserve Mines," in *Cape Breton's Magazine*, Number 16, June 1977.

Fowler, Bertram B., *The Lord Helps Those*. New York, Vanguard Press, 1938.

Hart, John, *History of Northeast Margaree*. Privately printed, 1963.

Laidlaw, Alexander Fraser, *The Campus and the Community: The Global Impact of the Antigonish Movement*. Montreal, Harvest House, 1961.

— "The Coady-Tompkins Experience." Remarks at the Coady-Tompkins Symposium, Scarborough Foreign Mission Society, Scarborough, Ont. March 10-11, 1978. Mimeo. 15 pp.

Lotz, Patricia A., *Scots in Groups: The Origin and Histo-*

ry of Scottish Societies with Particular Reference to Those Established in Nova Scotia. M.A. Thesis (Celtic Studies), St. Francis Xavier University, 1975.

— "The History of Library Development in the Atlantic Provinces," pp. 3-23 in Garry, Loraine Spencer and Carl (Eds.), *Canadian Libraries in their Changing Environment.* Downsview, York University, Centre for Continuing Education, 1977.

Lotz, Pat and Jim, *Cape Breton Island.* Vancouver, Douglas, David and Charles, 1974.

Lotz, Jim, and Michael R. Welton, "'Knowledge for the People': The Origins and Development of the Antigonish Movement," pp. 97-111 in Welton, Michael (Ed.), *Knowledge for the People.* Toronto, OISE Press, 1987.

MacDonald, J.D. Nelson, *Memoirs of an Unorthodox Clergyman.* Truro, Nova Scotia, Cooperative Resources, 1986.

MacKinnon, Richard, "Cooperativism and Vernacular Architecture in Tompkinsville," pp. 145-162 in Corbin, Carol and Judith Rolls (Eds.), *The Centre of the World at the Edge of a Continent.* Sydney, University College of Cape Breton Press, 1996.

MacLeod, Mary K., and James O. St. Clair, *Pride of Place: The Life and Times of Cape Breton Heritage Homes.* Sydney, University College of Cape Breton Press, 1994, pp. 167-174 "The Laben House," pp. 147-152 "The Dziubek House."

McKay, Ian, *The Quest of the Folk: Antimodernism and Cultural Selection in Twentieth Century Nova Scotia.* Montreal and Kingston, McGill-Queen's University Press, 1994.

Mellor, John, *The Company Store: James McLachlin and the Cape Breton Coal Miners, 1900-1925.* Toronto, Doubleday Canada Ltd, 1983.

Melnick, John, *Reserve Mines: A Brief History.* History Essay, Grade XII, 1978.

The People's School, Antigonish, N.S. January to March, 1921. Its purpose, its history, what the professors, the students, and the public say about it. n.a., n.p. 1921.

Report of the Royal Commission Investigating the Fisheries of the Maritime Provinces and Magdalen Islands, Ottawa, King's Printer, 1928.

A *Report* on the Proposed Federation of the Maritime University. Submitted to the Governors of St. Francis Xavier's College by a committee appointed by his Lordship Bishop Morrison, n.p. 1923.

Reid, John G., "Health, Education, Economy: Philanthropic Foundations in the Atlantic Region in the 1920s and 1930s," pp. 101-122 in McCann, Larry (Ed.), *People and Places: Studies of Small Town Life in the Maritimes.* Fredericton, N. B., Acadiensis Press, 1987.

Tompkins, Rev. Dr. J., *Knowledge for the People: A Call to St. Francis Xavier's College.* Antigonish, N. S., n.p. 1921.

Ward, Leo, *Nova Scotia: The Land of Co-operation.* New York, Sheed and Ward, 1942.

Welton, Michael R., "Bolsheviks of a Better Sort: Jimmy Tompkins and the Struggle for a People's Catholicism, 1908-1928," in *Proceedings*, Adult Education Research Conference, Edmonton, 1995.